44 It's a Small World
DISNEYLAND & MAGIC KINGDOM PARKS

46 Mickey Mouse March
THE MICKEY MOUSE CLUB

48 Supercalifragilisticexpialidocious
MARY POPPINS

52 Under the Sea
THE LITTLE MERMAID

59 I Just Can't Wait to Be King
THE LION KING

65 A Spoonful of Sugar
MARY POPPINS

68 When You Wish Upon a Star
PINOCCHIO

70 Whistle While You Work
SNOW WHITE AND THE SEVEN DWARFS

73 Who's Afraid of the Big Bad Wolf?
THREE LITTLE PIGS

76 Winnie the Pooh
THE MANY ADVENTURES OF WINNIE THE POOH

78 You've Got a Friend in Me
TOY STORY

82 Zip-A-Dee-Doo-Dah
SONG OF THE SOUTH

84 You'll Be in My Heart
TARZAN

87 BANJO NOTATION LEGEND

Baby Mine

from Walt Disney's DUMBO
Words by Ned Washington
Music by Frank Churchill

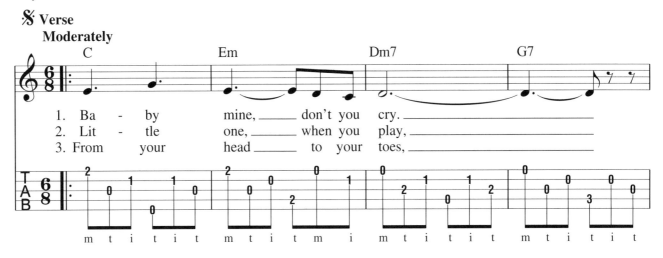

Key of C

Verse
Moderately

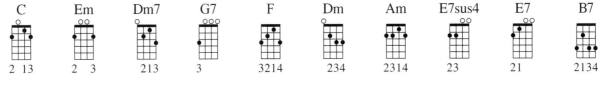
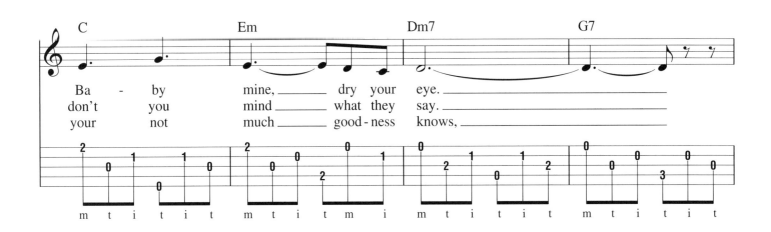

1. Ba - by mine, _____ don't you cry. _____
2. Lit - tle one, _____ when you play, _____
3. From your head _____ to your toes, _____

Ba - by mine, _____ dry your eye. _____
don't you mind _____ what they say. _____
your not much _____ good - ness knows, _____

To Coda

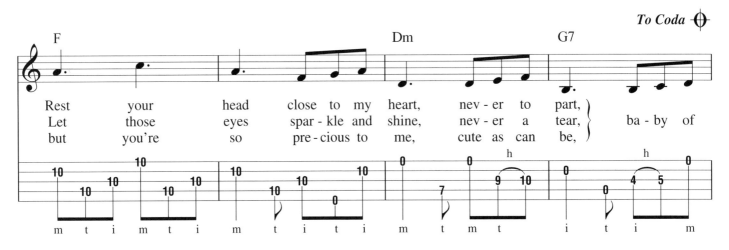

Rest your head close to my heart, nev - er to part, ⎱
Let those eyes spar - kle and shine, nev - er a tear, ⎰ ba - by of
but you're so pre - cious to me, cute as can be,

Copyright © 1941 by Walt Disney Productions
Copyright Renewed
This arrangement Copyright © 2012 by Walt Disney Productions
World Rights Controlled by Bourne Co. (ASCAP)
International Copyright Secured   All Rights Reserved

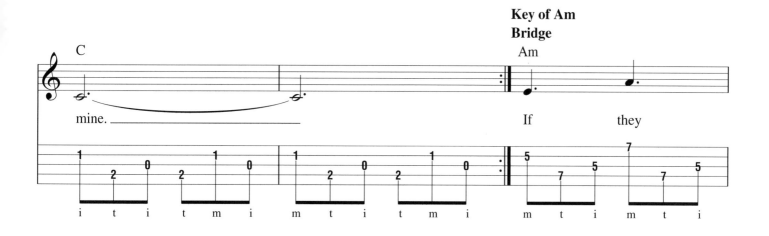

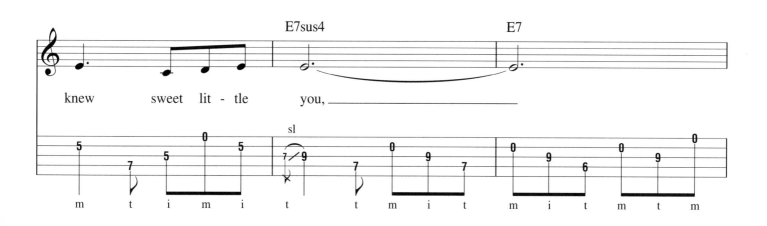

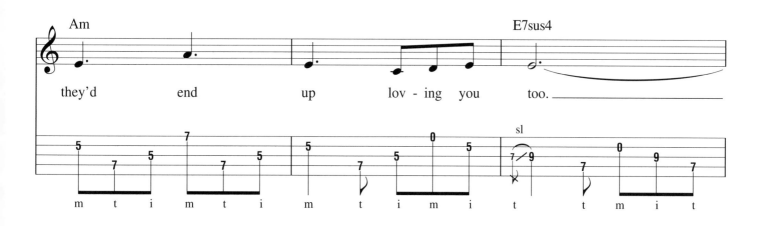

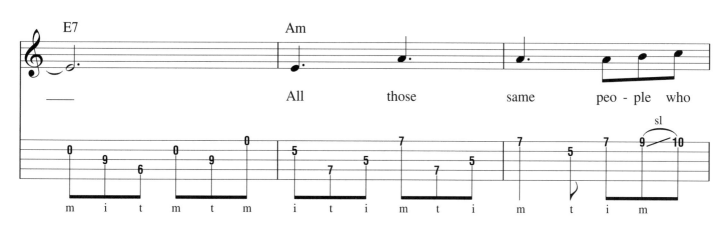

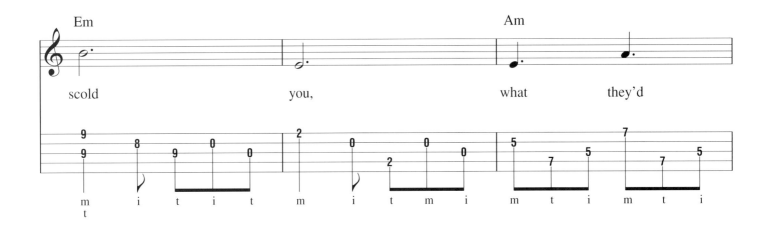

D.S. al Coda

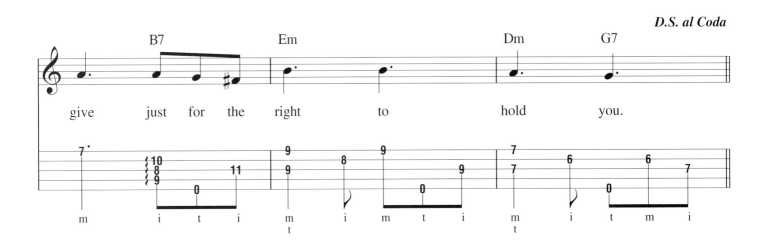

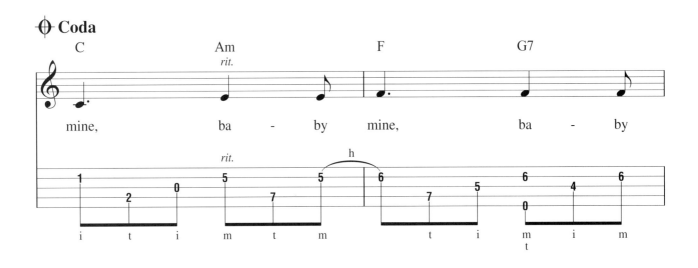

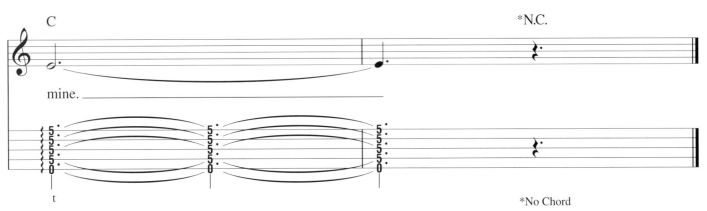

*No Chord

6

Disney Songs for Banjo

Arranged by Jim Schustedt

The following songs are the property of:
Bourne Co.
Music Publishers
5 West 37th Street
New York, NY 10018

BABY MINE
GIVE A LITTLE WHISTLE
HEIGH-HO
WHEN YOU WISH UPON A STAR
WHISTLE WHILE YOU WORK
WHO'S AFRAID OF THE BIG BAD WOLF?

Disney and Disney/Pixar characters and artwork © Disney Enterprises, Inc.

ISBN 978-1-61780-373-4

Walt Disney Music Company
Wonderland Music Company, Inc.

7777 W. BLUEMOUND RD. P.O. BOX 13819 MILWAUKEE, WI 53213

For all works contained herein:
Unauthorized copying, arranging, adapting, recording, Internet posting, public performance,
or other distribution of the printed music in this publication is an infringement of copyright.
Infringers are liable under the law.

Visit Hal Leonard Online at
www.halleonard.com

Contents

4 Baby Mine
DUMBO

7 Be Our Guest
BEAUTY AND THE BEAST

13 Bella Notte (This Is the Night)
LADY AND THE TRAMP

16 The Ballad of Davy Crockett
DAVY CROCKETT

18 The Bare Necessities
THE JUNGLE BOOK

22 Beauty and the Beast
BEAUTY AND THE BEAST

25 Colors of the Wind
POCAHONTAS

30 Bibbidi-Bobbidi-Boo (The Magic Song)
CINDERELLA

32 Chim Chim Cher-ee
MARY POPPINS

36 Cruella de Vil
101 DALMATIONS

39 Heigh-Ho
SNOW WHITE AND THE SEVEN DWARFS

42 Give a Little Whistle
PINOCCHIO

Be Our Guest

from Walt Disney's BEAUTY AND THE BEAST
Lyrics by Howard Ashman
Music by Alan Menken

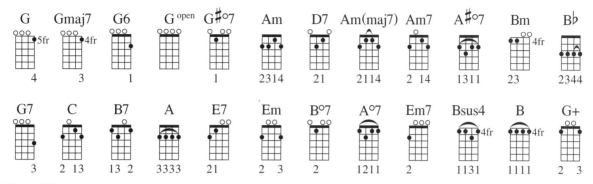

Key of G

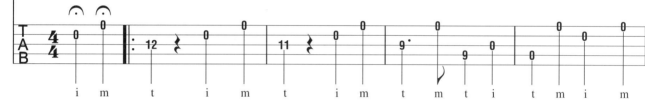

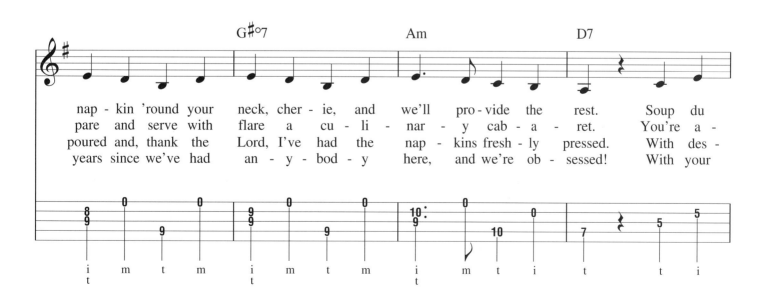

© 1991 Walt Disney Music Company and Wonderland Music Company, Inc.
This arrangement © 2012 Walt Disney Music Company and Wonderland Music Company, Inc.
All Rights Reserved   Used by Permission

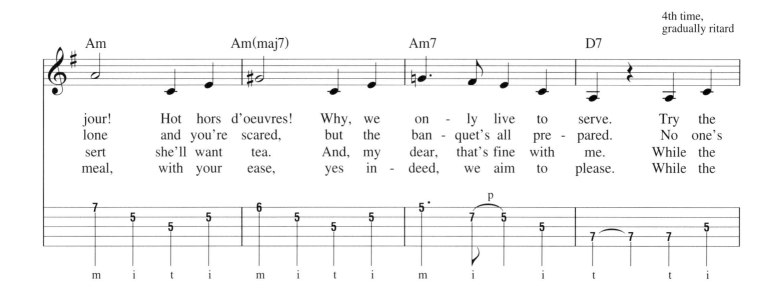

4th time,
gradually ritard

| Am | Am(maj7) | Am7 | D7 |

jour!   Hot   hors   d'oeuvres!   Why,   we   on - ly   live   to   serve.   Try   the
lone   and   you're   scared,   but   the   ban - quet's   all   pre - pared.   No   one's
sert   she'll   want   tea.   And,   my   dear,   that's   fine   with   me.   While   the
meal,   with   your   ease,   yes   in - deed,   we   aim   to   please.   While   the

4th time, To Coda 1 〇

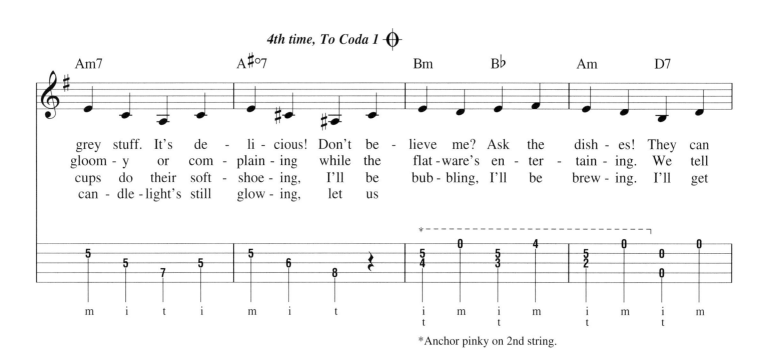

| Am7 | A♯°7 | Bm | B♭ | Am | D7 |

grey   stuff.   It's   de - li - cious!   Don't   be - lieve   me?   Ask   the   dish - es!   They   can
gloom - y   or   com - plain - ing   while   the   flat - ware's   en - ter - tain - ing.   We   tell
cups   do   their   soft - shoe - ing,   I'll   be   bub - bling,   I'll   be   brew - ing.   I'll   get
can - dle -light's   still   glow - ing,   let   us

*Anchor pinky on 2nd string.

𝄋 𝄋

4th time, Very slow & gradually accelerate

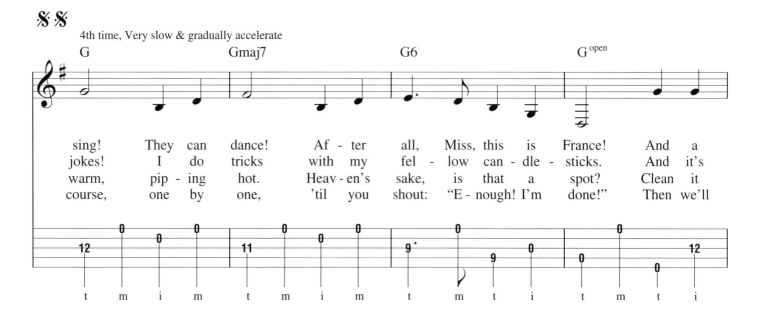

| G | Gmaj7 | G6 | G^open |

sing!   They   can   dance!   Af - ter   all,   Miss,   this   is   France!   And   a
jokes!   I   do   tricks   with   my   fel - low   can - dle - sticks.   And   it's
warm,   pip - ing   hot.   Heav - en's   sake,   is   that   a   spot?   Clean   it
course,   one   by   one,   'til   you   shout: "E - nough!   I'm   done!"   Then   we'll

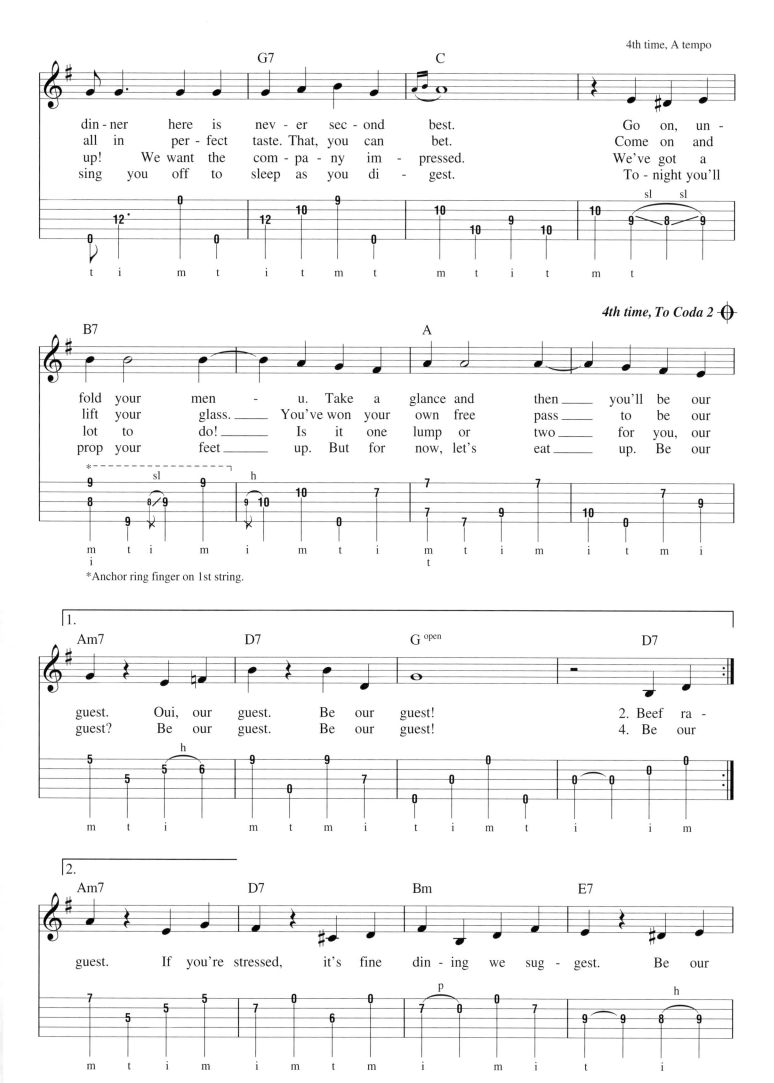

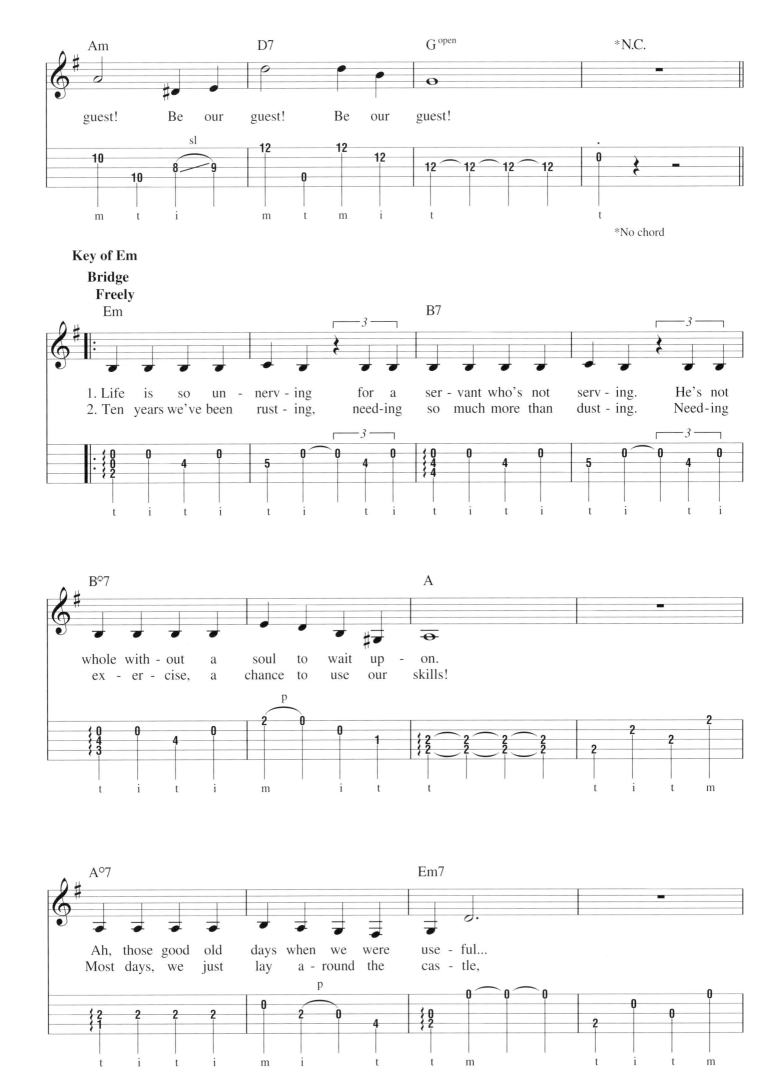

*No chord

Key of Em

Bridge

Freely

10

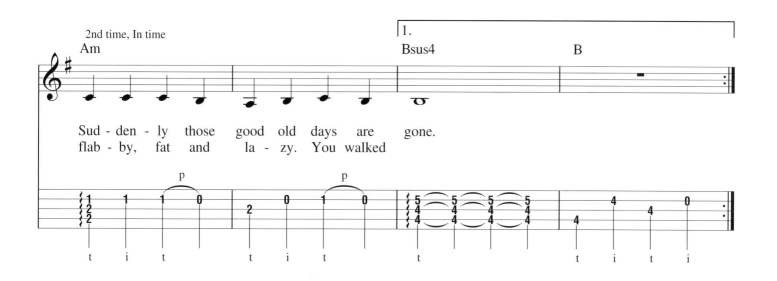

Sud - den - ly those good old days are gone.
flab - by, fat and la - zy. You walked

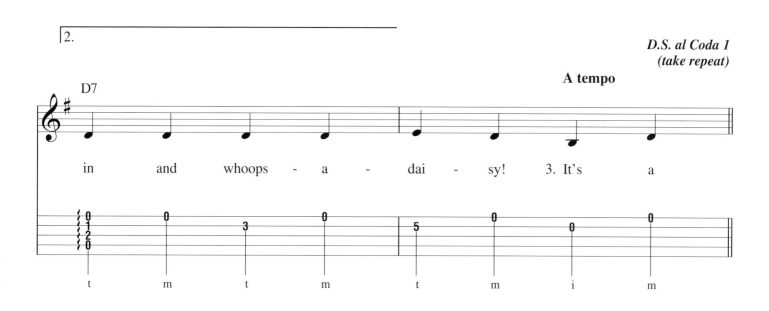

in and whoops - a - dai - sy! 3. It's a

D.S. al Coda 1
(take repeat)

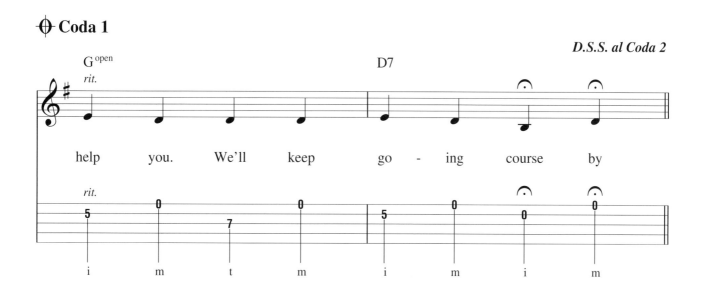

help you. We'll keep go - ing course by

Coda 2

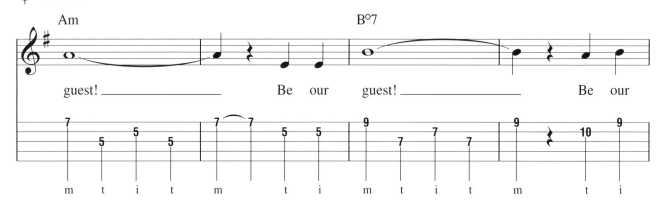

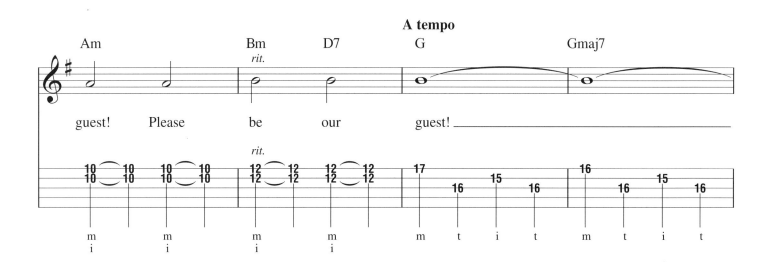

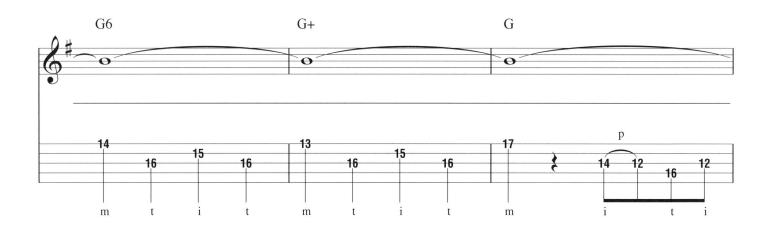

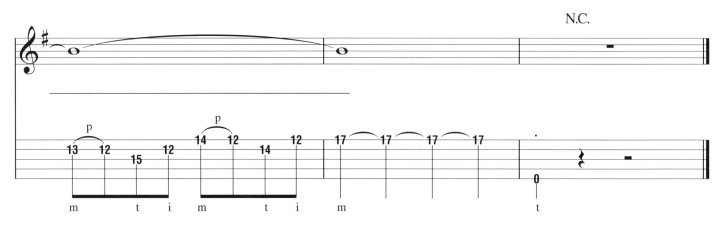

Bella Notte
(This Is the Night)

from Walt Disney's LADY AND THE TRAMP
Words and Music by Peggy Lee and Sonny Burke

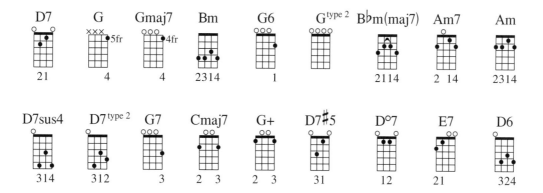

Key of G

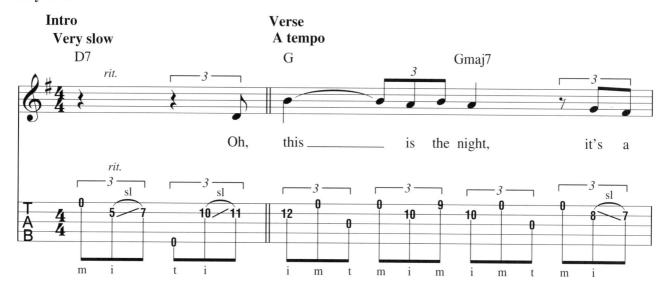

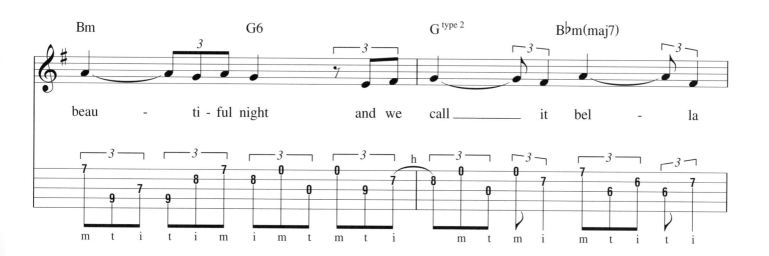

© 1952 Walt Disney Music Company
Copyright Renewed
This arrangement © 2012 Walt Disney Music Company
All Rights Reserved   Used by Permission

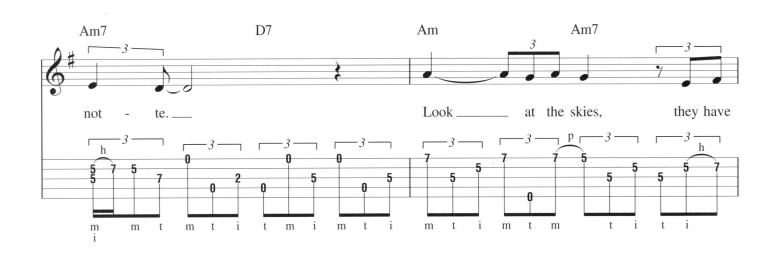

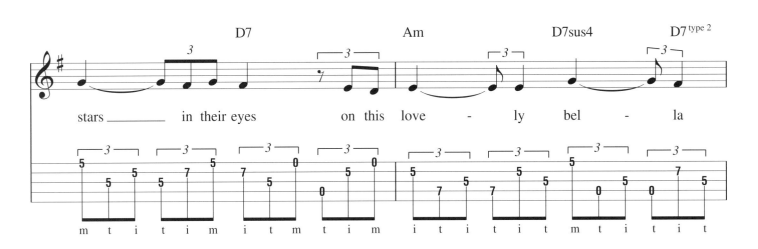

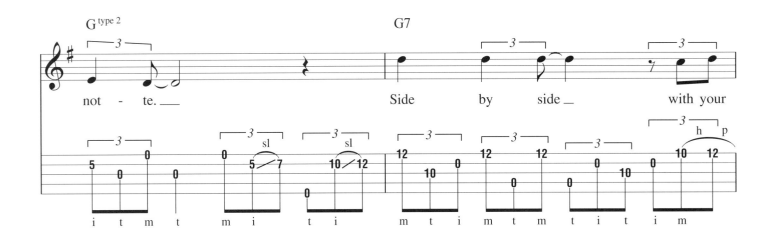

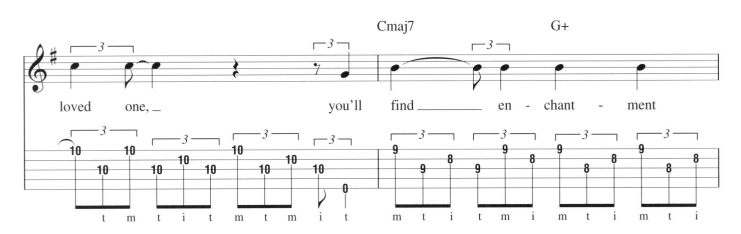

The Ballad of Davy Crockett

from Walt Disney's DAVY CROCKETT
Words by Tom Blackburn
Music by George Bruns

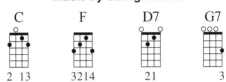

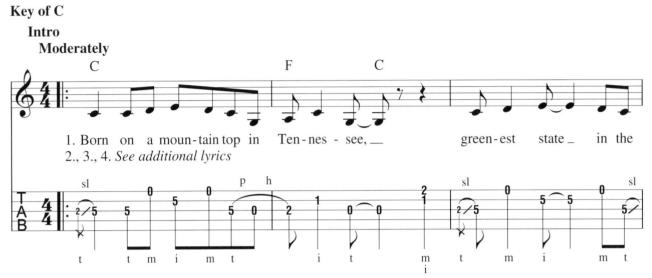

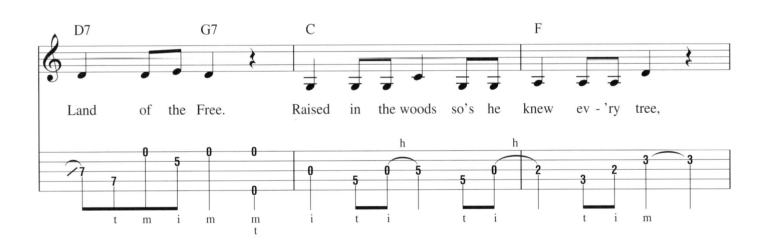

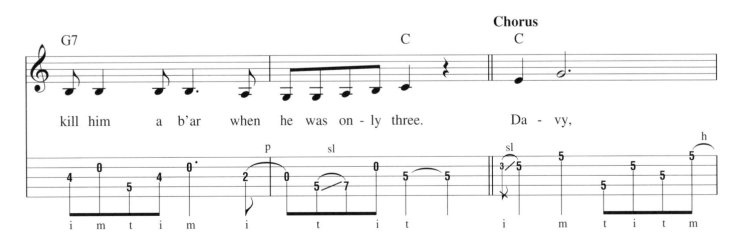

© 1954 Wonderland Music Company, Inc.
Copyright Renewed
This arrangement © 2012 Wonderland Music Company, Inc.
All Rights Reserved   Used by Permission

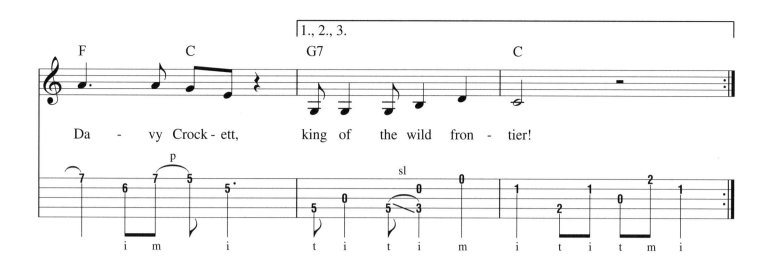

Da - vy Crock - ett, king of the wild fron - tier!

4.

Slower

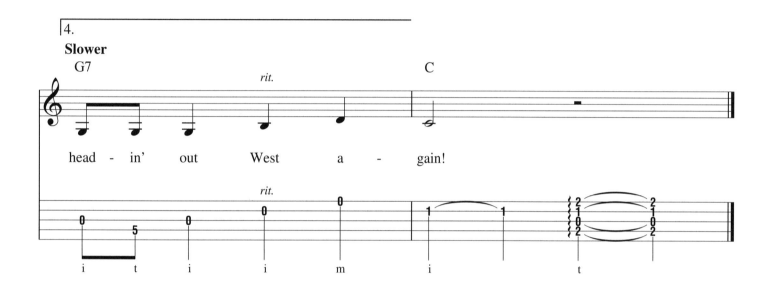

head - in' out West a - gain!

Additional Lyrics

2. Fought single-handed through the Injun War
   Till the Creeks was whipped and peace was in store.
   And while he was handlin' this risky chore
   Made his-self a legend forevermore.

   Davy, Davy Crockett,
   The man who don't know fear.

3. He went off to Congress and he served a spell
   Fixin' up the government and laws as well.
   Took over Washington so we heard tell
   And patched up the crack in the Liberty Bell.

   Davy, Davy Crockett,
   Seein' his duty clear.

4. When he'd come home, his politickin' done,
   The western march had just begun.
   So he packed his gear and his trusty gun,
   And lit out a grinnin' to follow the sun.

   Davy, Davy Crockett,
   Headin' out West again!

The Bare Necessities

from Walt Disney's THE JUNGLE BOOK

Words and Music by Terry Gilkyson

© 1964 Wonderland Music Company, Inc.
Copyright Renewed
This arrangement © 2012 Wonderland Music Company, Inc.
All Rights Reserved   Used by Permission

Bridge

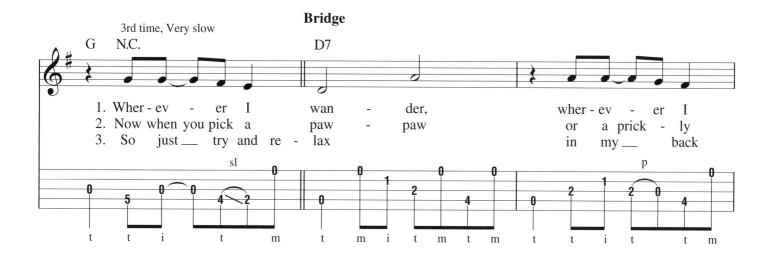

1. Wher - ev - er I wan - der, wher - ev - er I
2. Now when you pick a paw - paw or a prick - ly
3. So just try and re - lax in my back

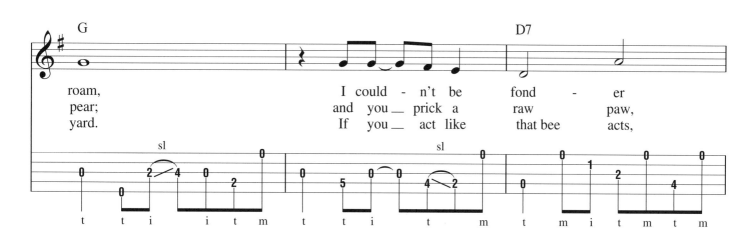

roam,
pear;
yard.

I could - n't be fond - er
and you prick a raw paw,
If you act like that bee acts,

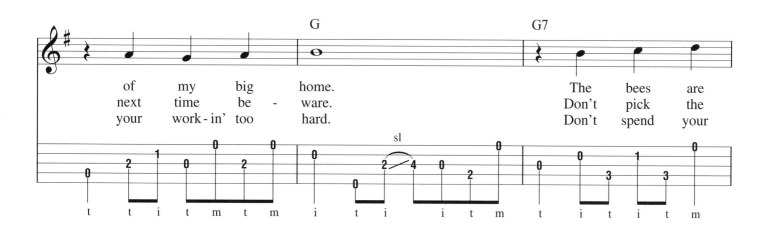

of my big home.
next time be - ware.
your work - in' too hard.

The bees are
Don't pick the
Don't spend your

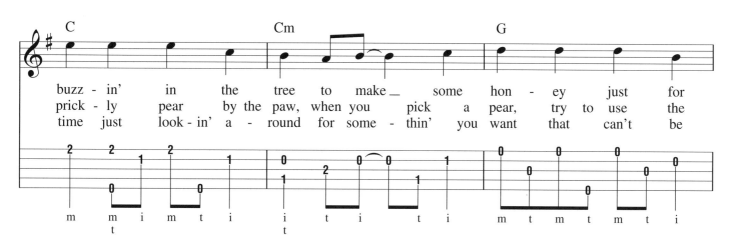

buzz - in' in the tree to make some hon - ey just for
prick - ly pear by the paw, when you pick a pear, try to use for the
time just look - in' a - round for some - thin' you want that can't be

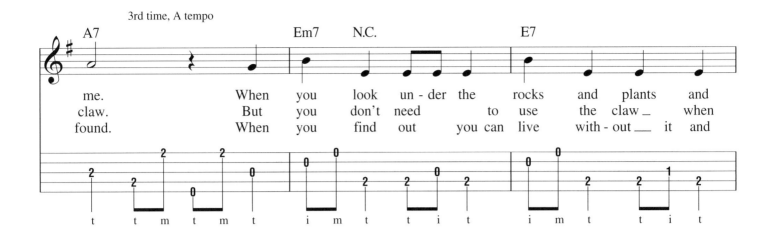

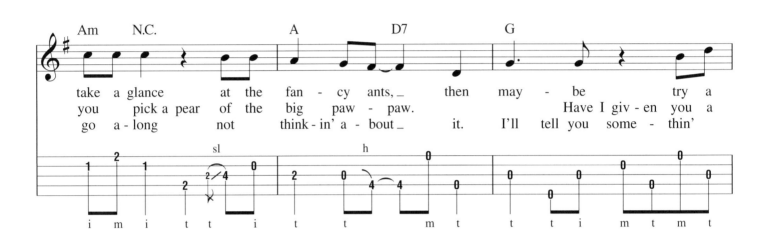

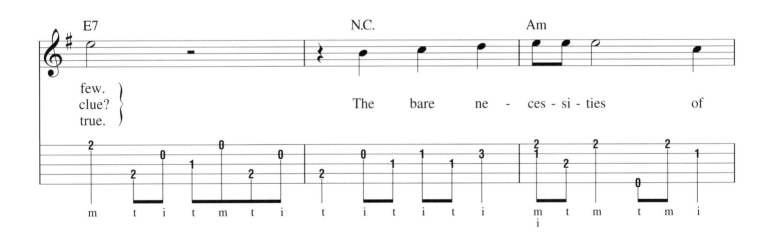

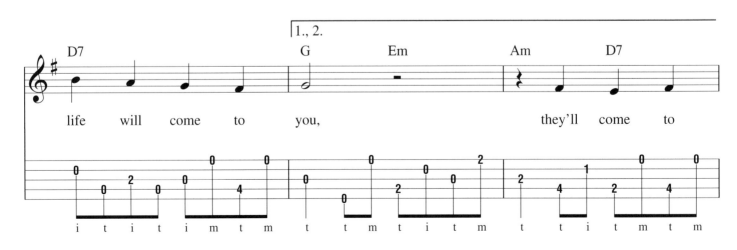

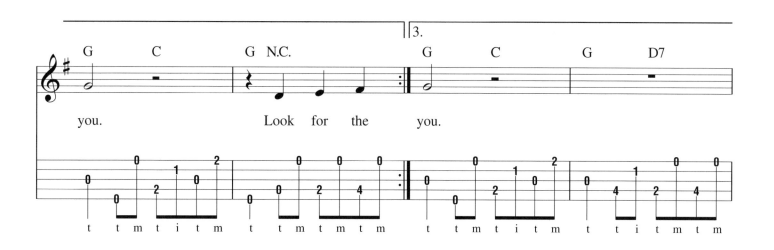

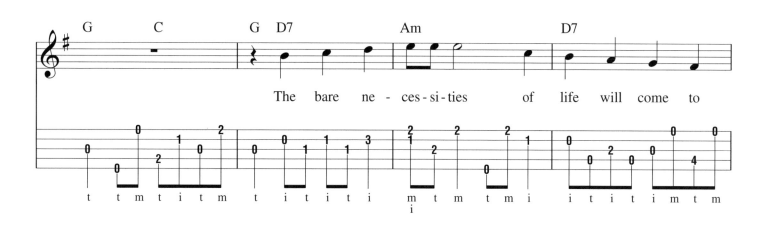

D.S. al Coda

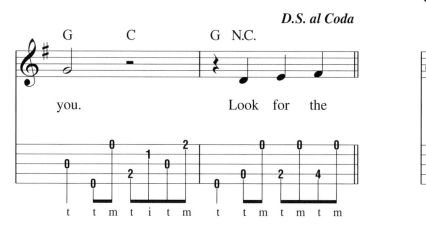

⊕ Coda

Outro-Tag

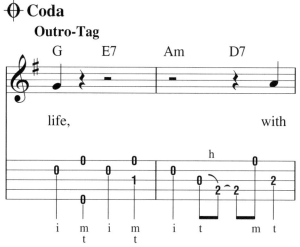

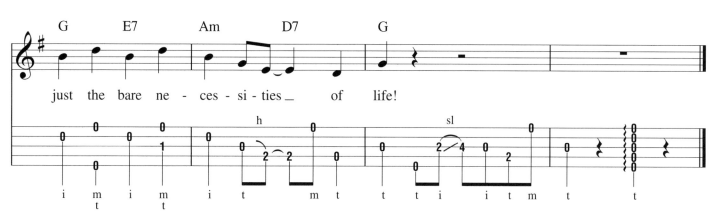

Beauty and the Beast

from Walt Disney's BEAUTY AND THE BEAST

Lyrics by Howard Ashman
Music by Alan Menken

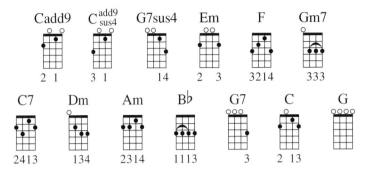

Key of C

Intro
Moderately slow

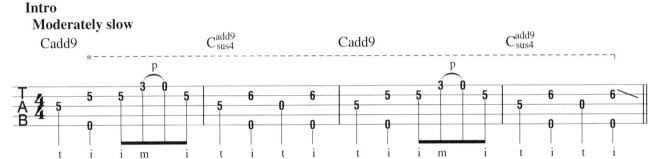

*Keep pinky on 2nd string.

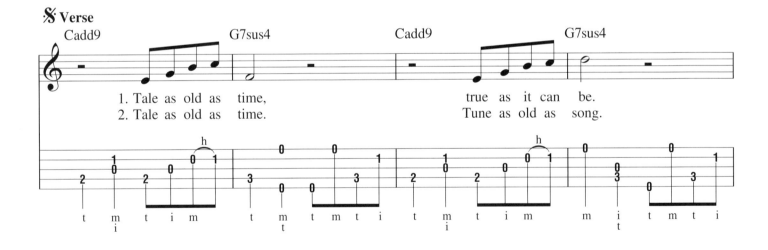

1. Tale as old as time, true as it can be.
2. Tale as old as time. Tune as old as song.

Bare-ly e-ven friends, then some-bod-y bends un-ex-pect-ed-ly.
Bit-ter-sweet and strange, find-ing you can change, learn-ing you were wrong.

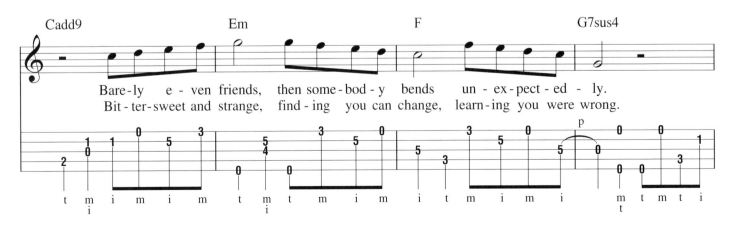

© 1991 Walt Disney Music Company and Wonderland Music Company, Inc.
This arrangement © 2012 Walt Disney Music Company and Wonderland Music Company, Inc.
All Rights Reserved   Used by Permission

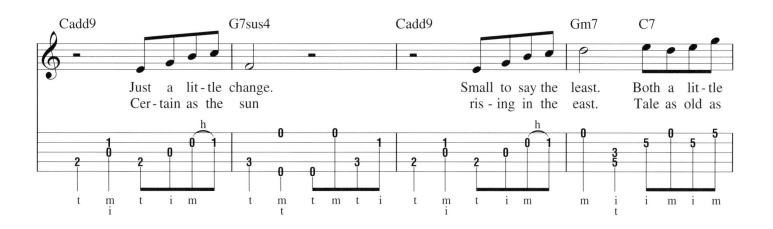

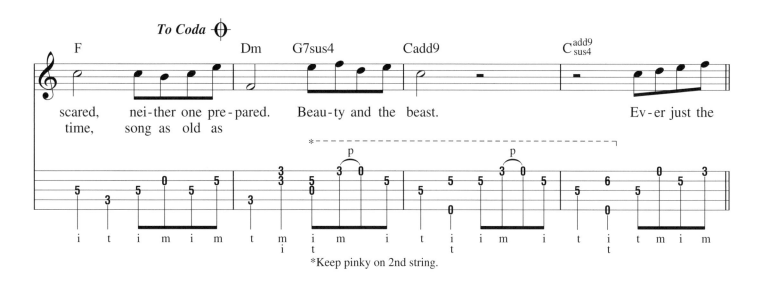

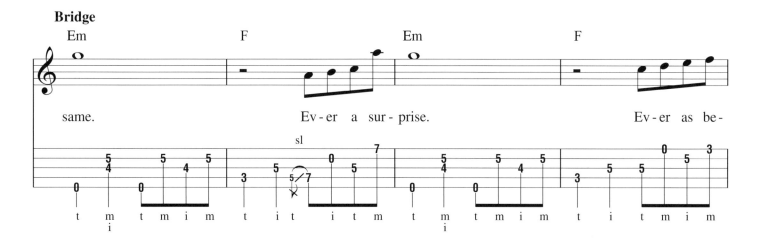

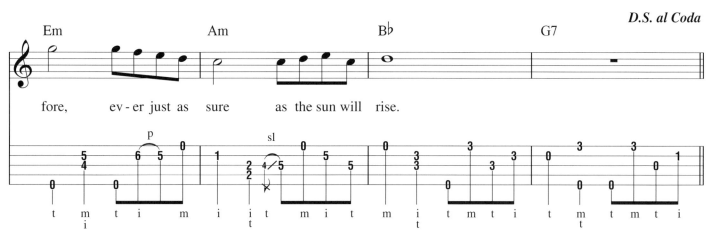

Coda

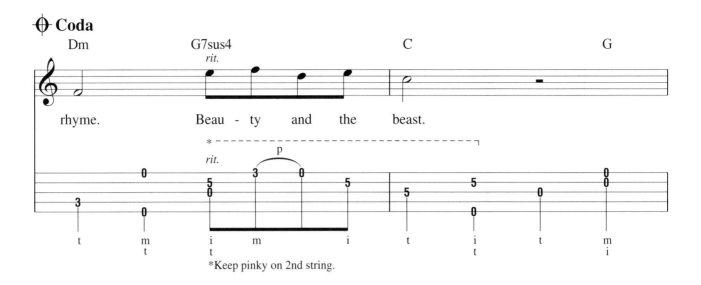

rhyme.   Beau - ty   and   the   beast.

*Keep pinky on 2nd string.

Slower

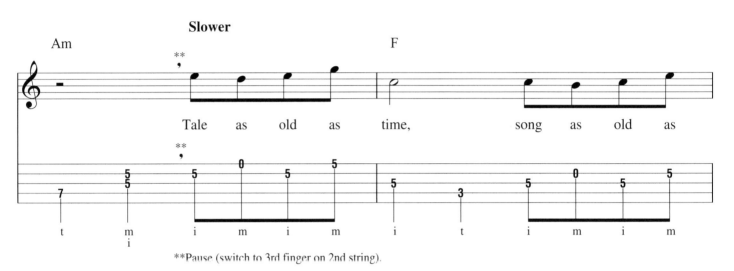

Tale   as   old   as   time,   song   as   old   as

**Pause (switch to 3rd finger on 2nd string).

Outro
A tempo

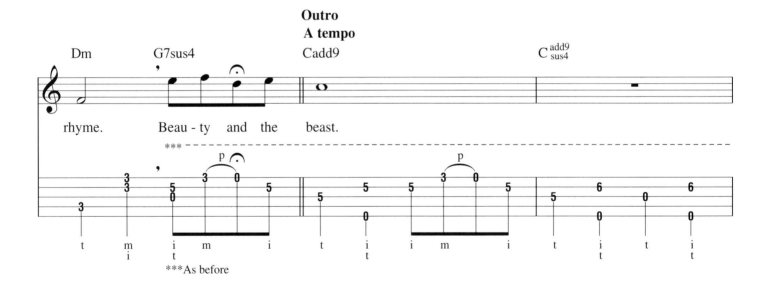

rhyme.   Beau - ty   and   the   beast.

***As before

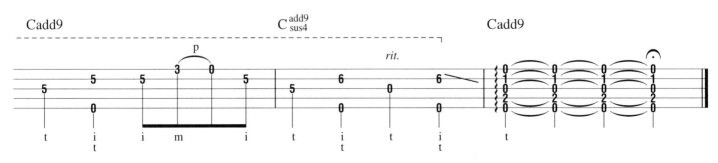

Colors of the Wind

from Walt Disney's POCAHONTAS

Music by Alan Menken

Lyrics by Stephen Schwartz

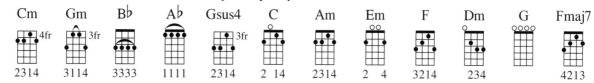

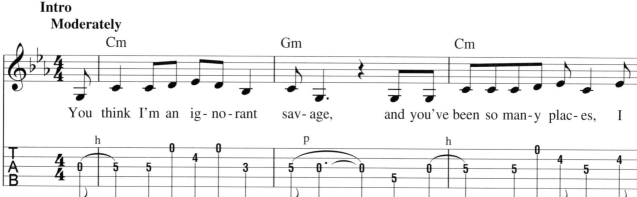

Key of Cm

Intro

Moderately

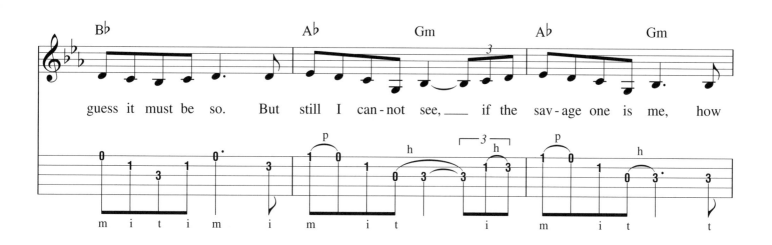

You think I'm an ig-no-rant sav-age, and you've been so man-y plac-es, I

guess it must be so. But still I can-not see, ___ if the sav-age one is me, how

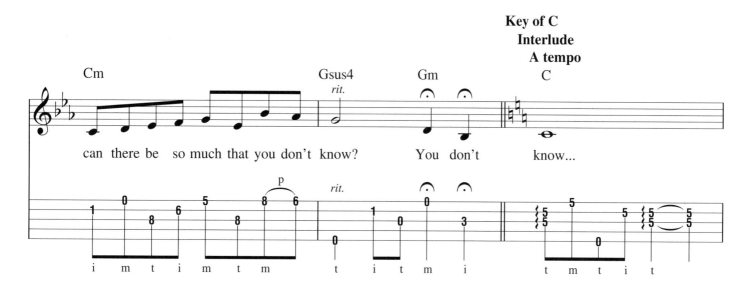

can there be so much that you don't know? You don't know...

Key of C

Interlude

A tempo

© 1995 Wonderland Music Company, Inc. and Walt Disney Music Company
This arrangement © 2012 Wonderland Music Company, Inc. and Walt Disney Music Company
All Rights Reserved   Used by Permission

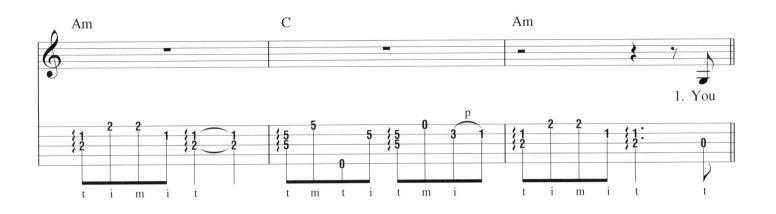

1. You

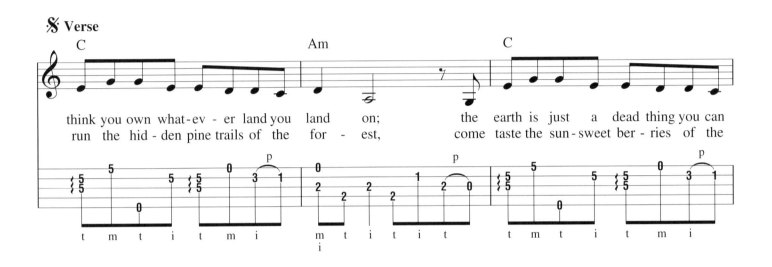

𝄋 Verse

think you own what-ev - er land you land on;　the earth is just　a　dead thing you can
run the hid - den pine trails of the　for - est,　come taste the sun - sweet ber - ries of the

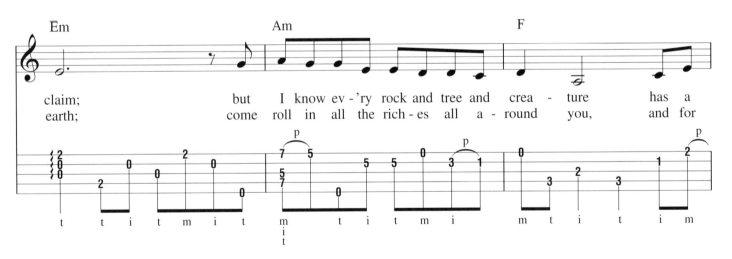

claim;　but I know ev -'ry rock and tree and crea - ture　has a
earth;　come roll in all the rich - es all a - round　you,　and for

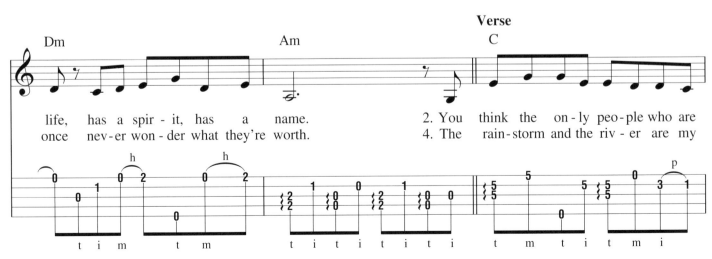

life, has a spir - it, has　a　name.　2. You think the on - ly peo - ple who are
once nev - er won - der what they're worth.　4. The rain - storm and the riv - er are my

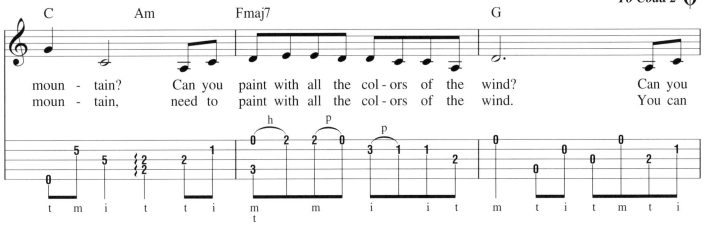

Interlude
A tempo

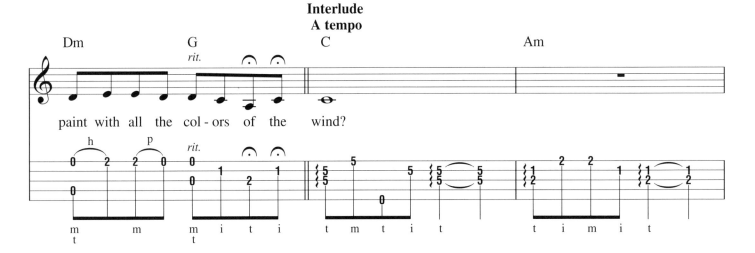

D.S. al Coda 1

Coda 1

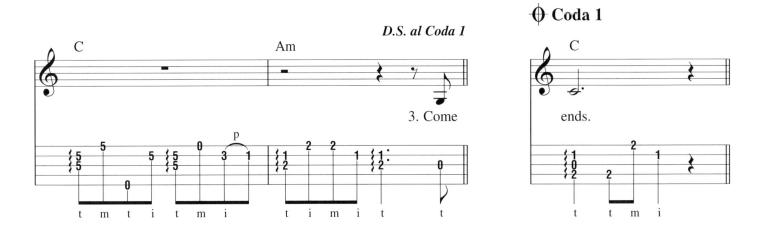

Bridge

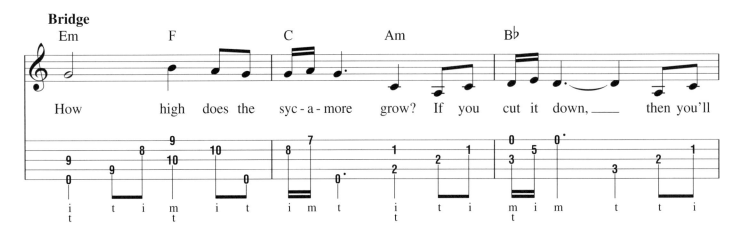

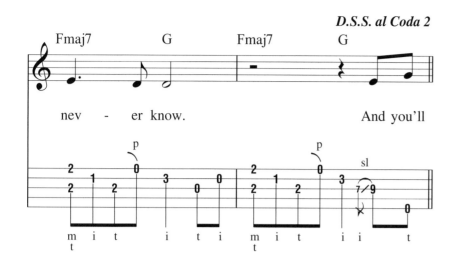

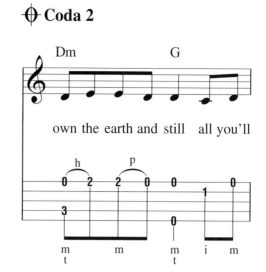

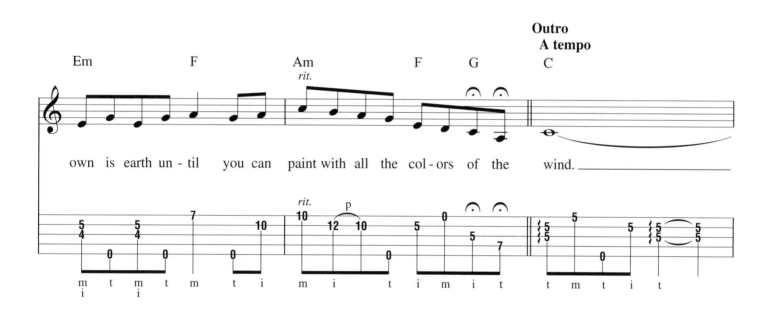

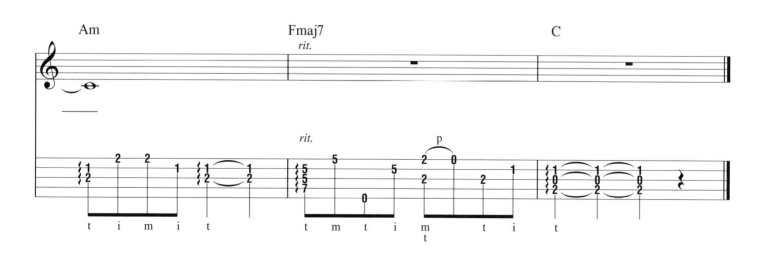

Bibbidi-Bobbidi-Boo
(The Magic Song)

from Walt Disney's CINDERELLA
Words by Jerry Livingston
Music by Mack David and Al Hoffman

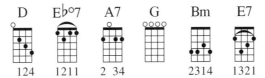

Key of D

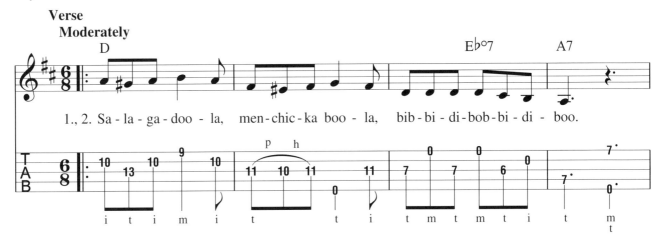

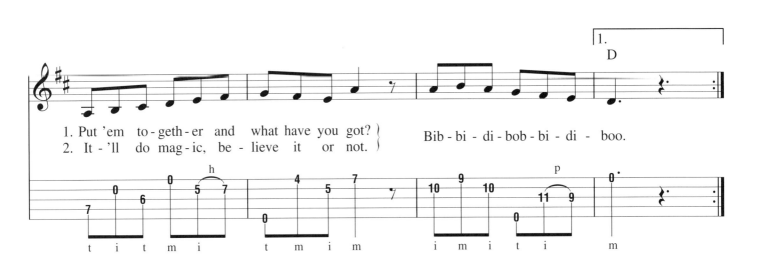

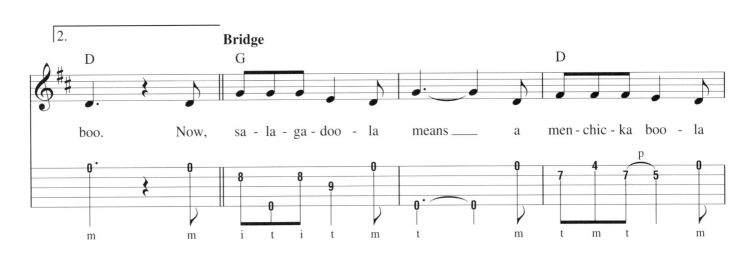

© 1948 Walt Disney Music Company
Copyright Renewed
This arrangement © 2012 Walt Disney Music Company
All Rights Reserved   Used by Permission

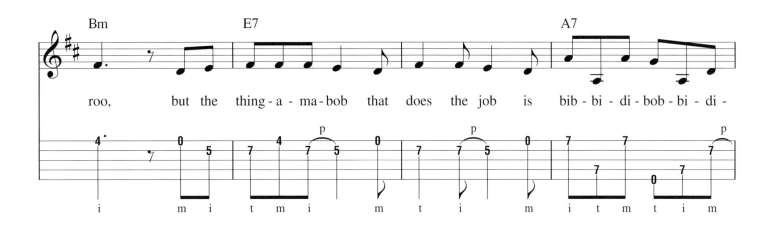

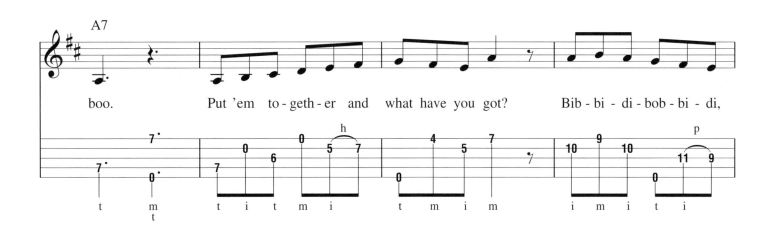

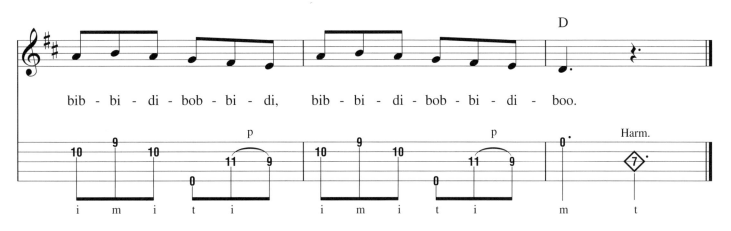

Chim Chim Cher-ee

from Walt Disney's MARY POPPINS
Words and Music by Richard M. Sherman and Robert B. Sherman

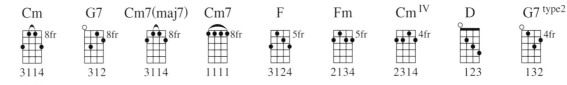

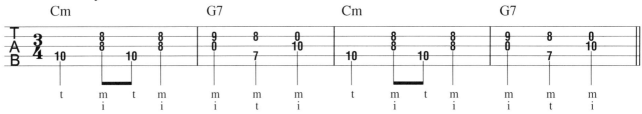

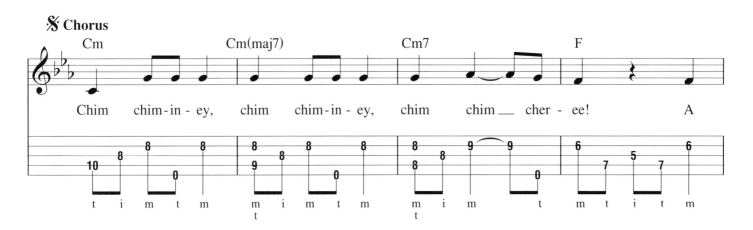

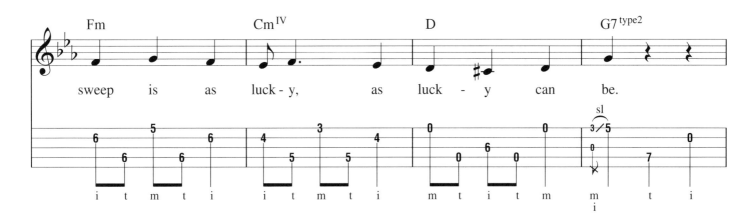

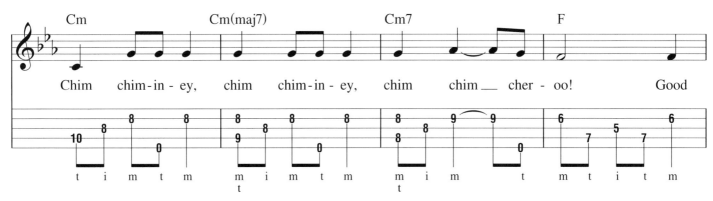

© 1963 Wonderland Music Company, Inc.
Copyright Renewed
This arrangement © 2012 Wonderland Music Company, Inc.
All Rights Reserved   Used by Permission

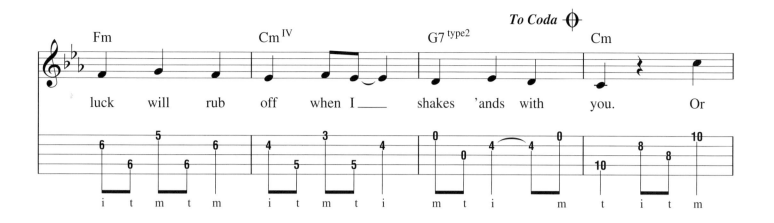

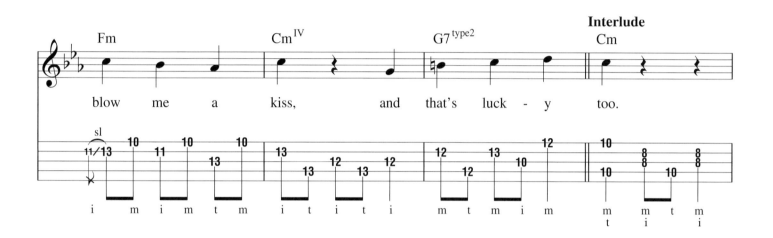

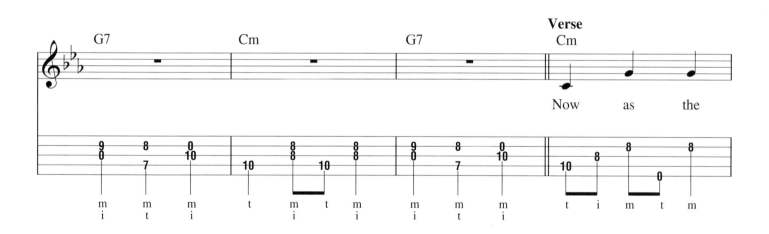

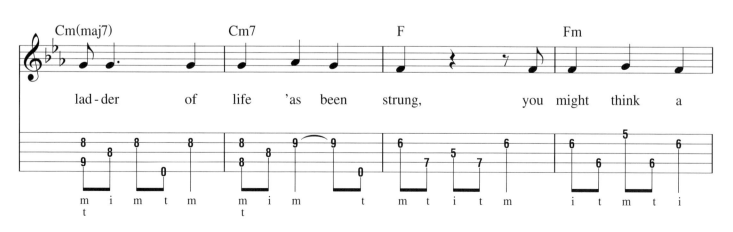

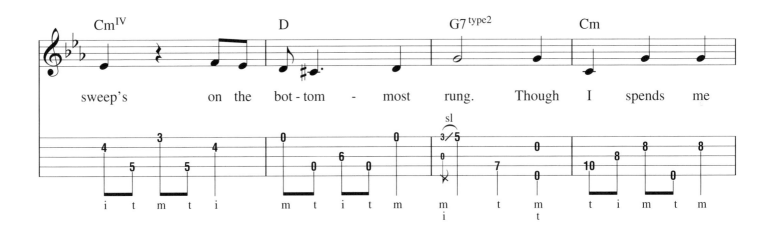

sweep's on the bot - tom - most rung. Though I spends me

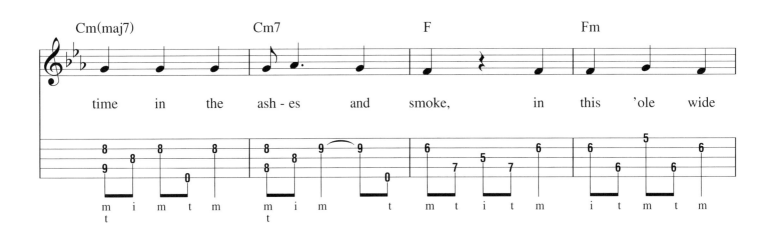

time in the ash - es and smoke, in this 'ole wide

D.S. al Coda

⊕ **Coda**

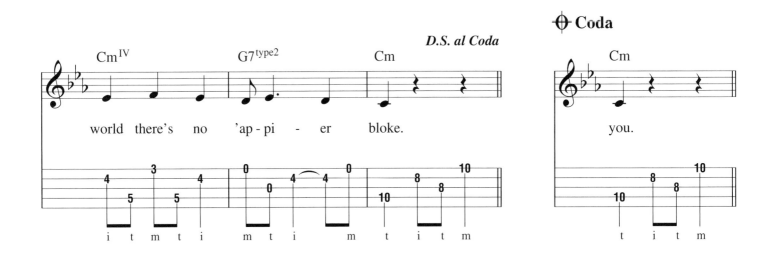

world there's no 'ap - pi - er bloke.

you.

Chorus

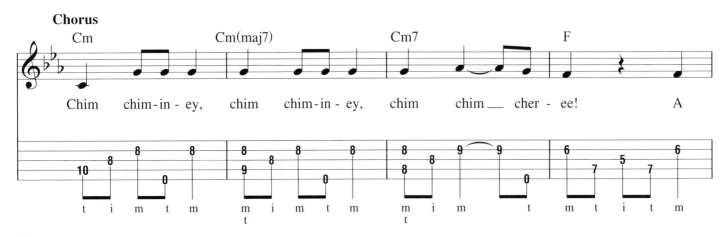

Chim chim-in - ey, chim chim-in - ey, chim chim ___ cher - ee! A

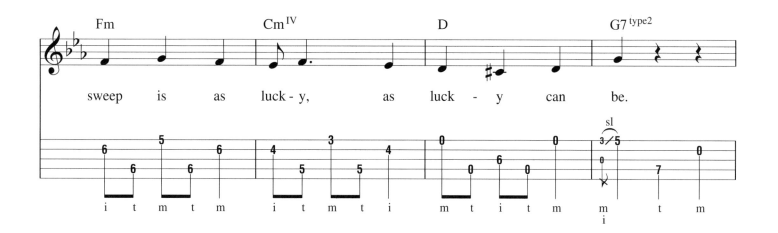

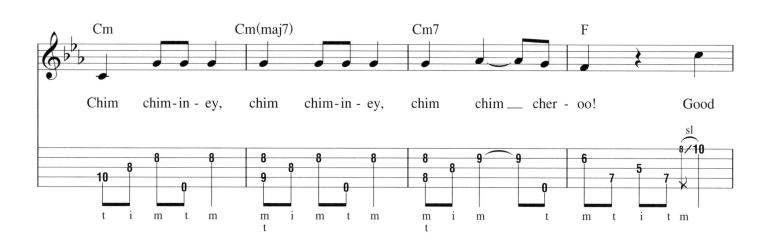

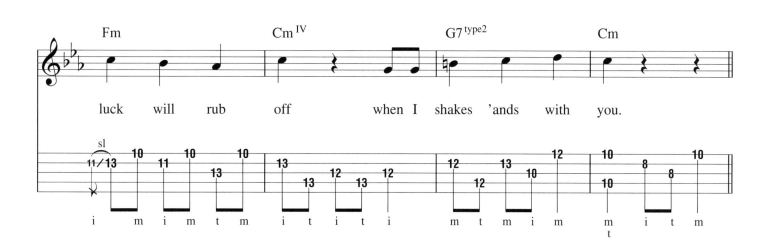

Outro-Tag

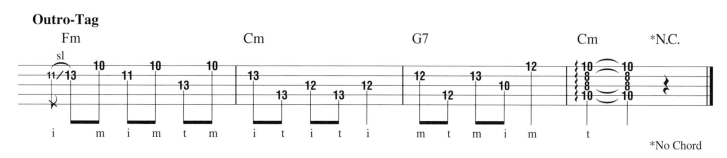

*No Chord

Cruella de Vil

from Walt Disney's 101 DALMATIANS
Words and Music by Mel Leven

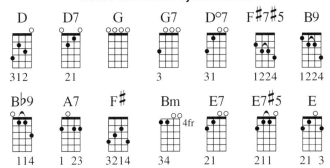

Key of D

Moderate swing

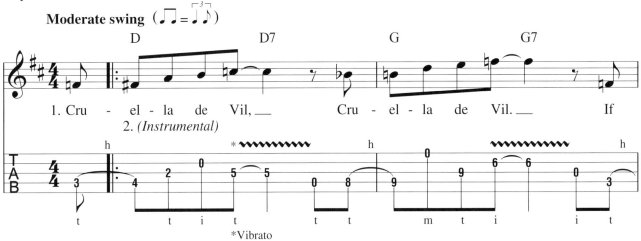

1. Cru - el - la de Vil, ___ Cru - el - la de Vil. ___ If
2. *(Instrumental)*

*Vibrato

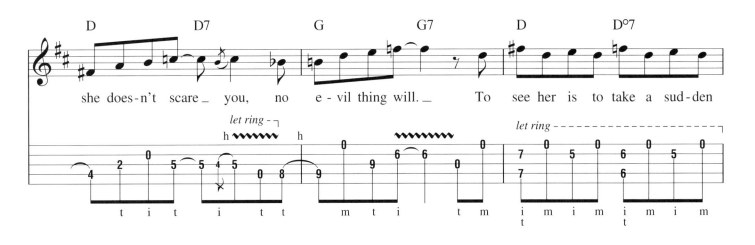

she does-n't scare ___ you, no e - vil thing will. ___ To see her is to take a sud - den

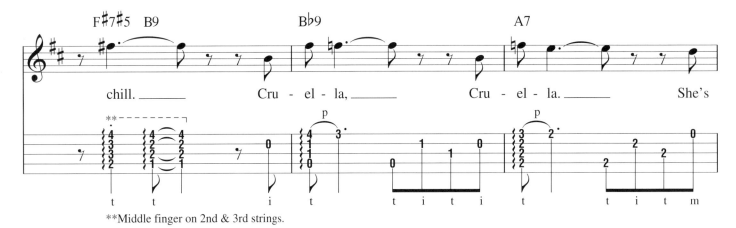

chill. ___ Cru - el - la, ___ Cru - el - la. ___ She's

**Middle finger on 2nd & 3rd strings.

© 1959 Walt Disney Music Company
Copyright Renewed
This arrangement © 2012 Walt Disney Music Company
All Rights Reserved   Used by Permission

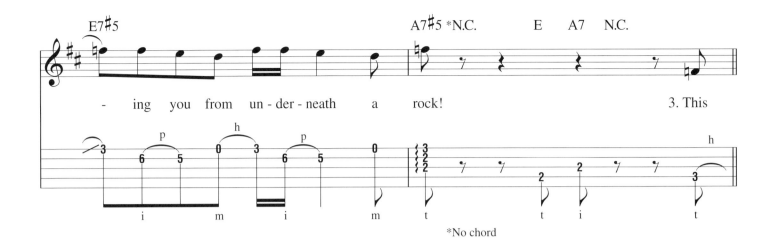

-ing you from un-der-neath a rock! 3. This

*No chord

Verse

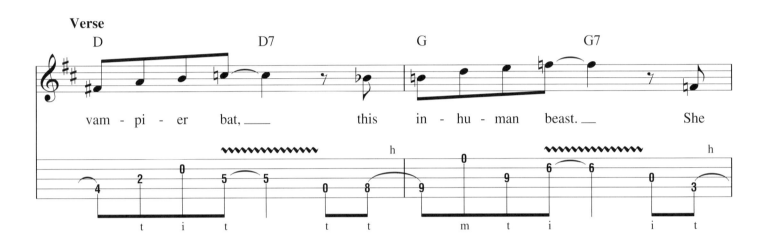

vam-pi-er bat, _____ this in-hu-man beast. __ She

ought-a be locked _ up and nev-er re-leased. _ The world was such a whole-some place un-

let ring

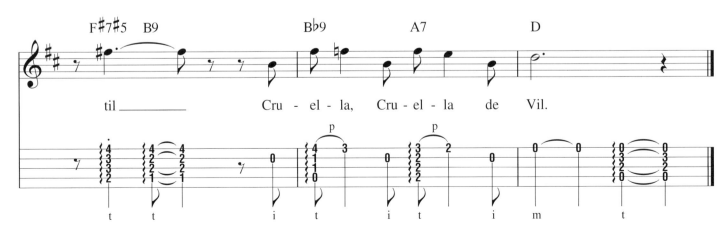

til _____ Cru-el-la, Cru-el-la de Vil.

Heigh-Ho

The Dwarfs' Marching Song from Walt Disney's SNOW WHITE AND THE SEVEN DWARFS
Words by Larry Morey
Music by Frank Churchill

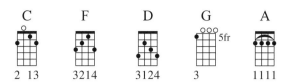

Key of C

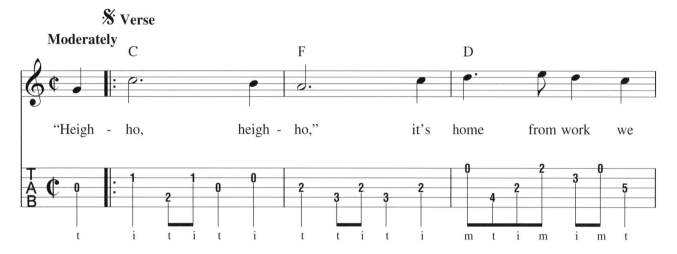

"Heigh - ho, heigh - ho," it's home from work we

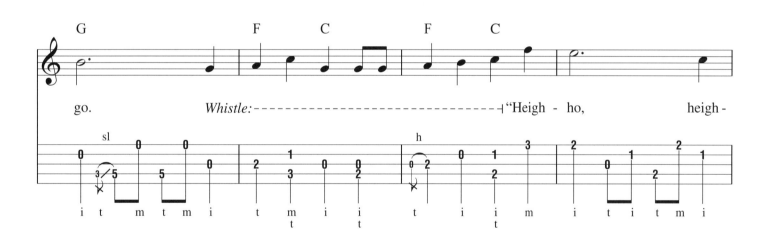

go. *Whistle:* - "Heigh - ho, heigh -

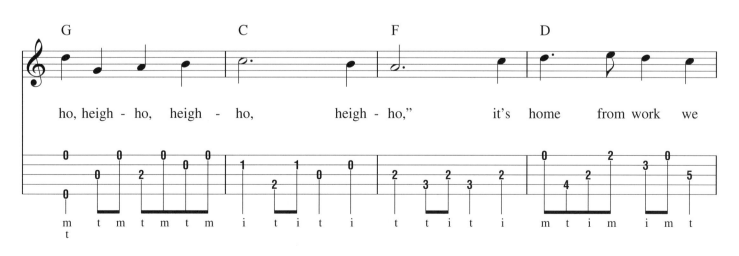

ho, heigh - ho, heigh ho, heigh - ho," it's home from work we

Copyright © 1938 by Bourne Co. (ASCAP)
Copyright Renewed
This arrangement Copyright © 2012 by Bourne Co.
International Copyright Secured   All Rights Reserved

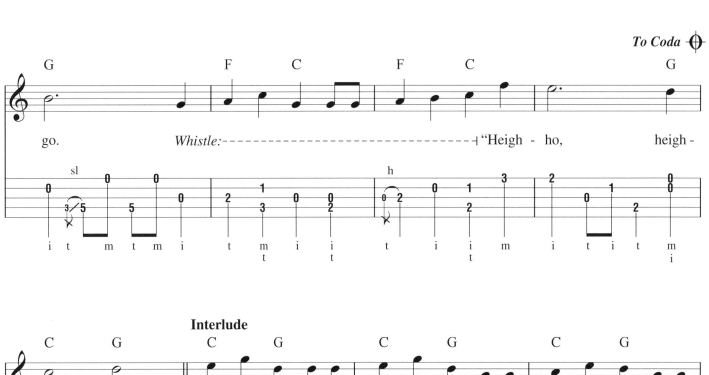

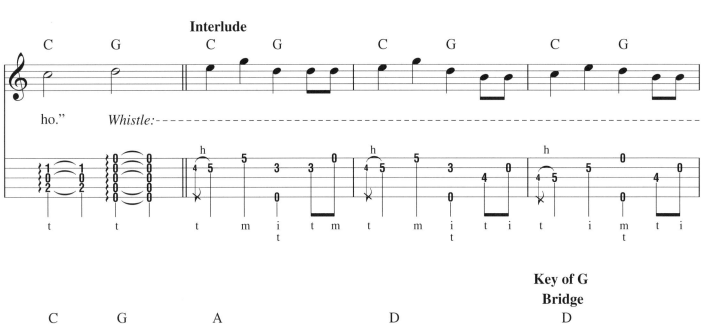

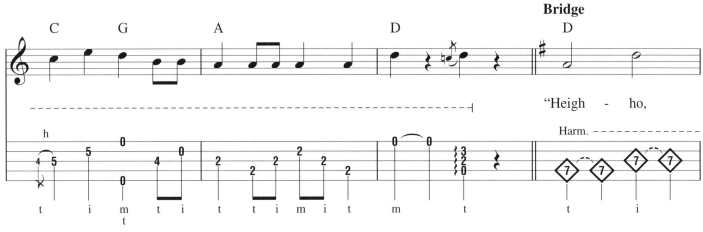

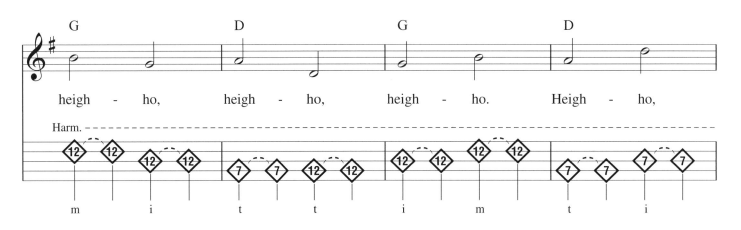

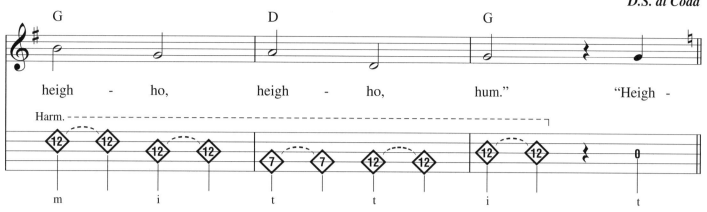

heigh - ho,   heigh - ho,   hum."   "Heigh -

Coda

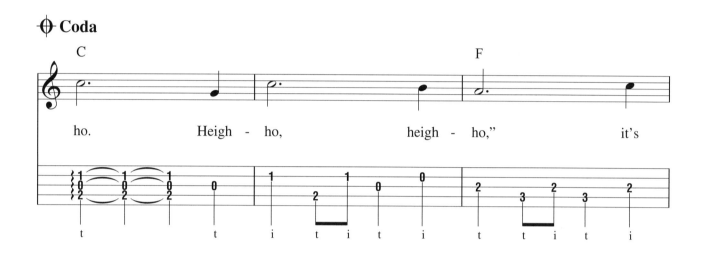

ho.   Heigh - ho,   heigh - ho,"   it's

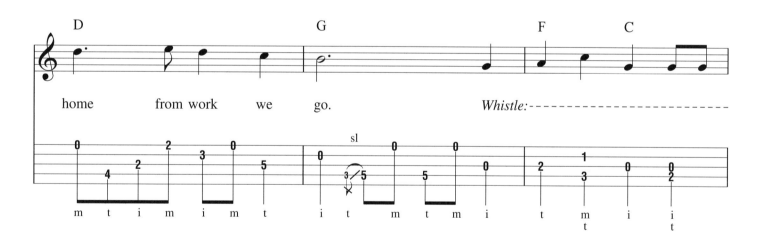

home   from work   we   go.   *Whistle:*- - - - - - - - - - - - - - - -

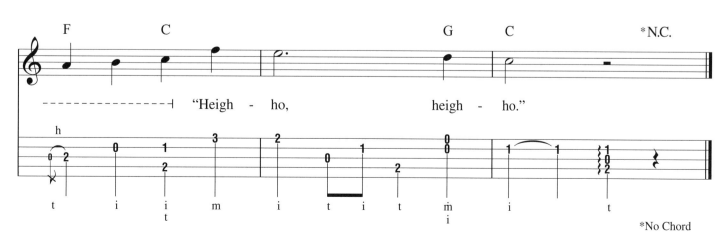

- - - - - - - - - - - -   "Heigh - ho,   heigh - ho."

*No Chord

Give a Little Whistle

from Walt Disney's PINOCCHIO
Words by Ned Washington
Music by Leigh Harline

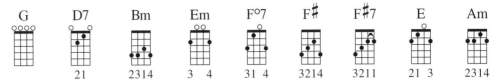

Key of G

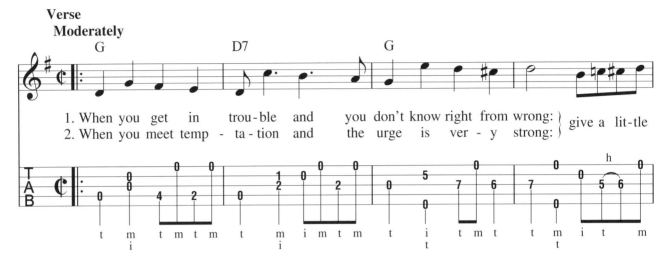

1. When you get in trou-ble and you don't know right from wrong: } give a lit-tle
2. When you meet temp - ta-tion and the urge is ver - y strong: } give a lit-tle

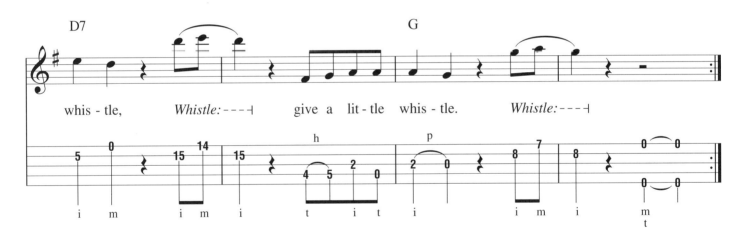

whis - tle, *Whistle:* - - - give a lit-tle whis - tle. *Whistle:* - - -

Key of Bm
Bridge

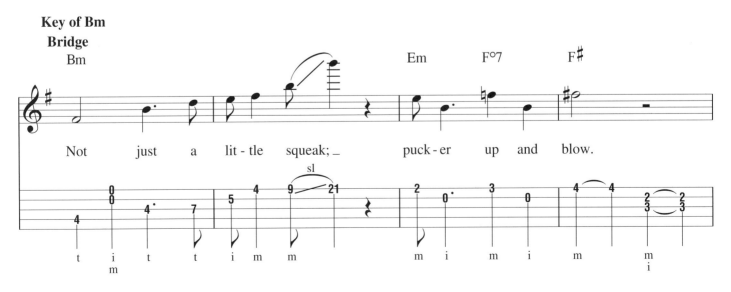

Not just a lit-tle squeak; puck - er up and blow.

Copyright © 1940 by BOURNE CO. (ASCAP)
Copyright Renewed
This arrangement Copyright © 2012 by Bourne Co.
International Copyright Secured   All Rights Reserved

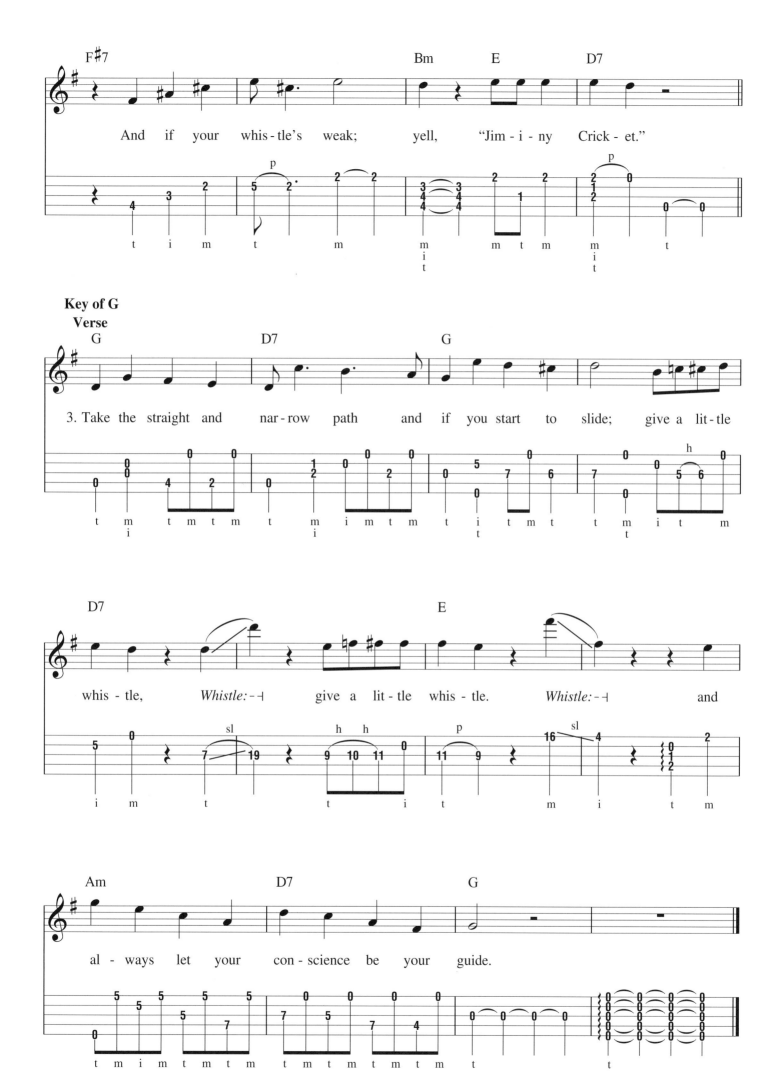

It's a Small World

from Disneyland Resort® and Magic Kingdom® Park
Words and Music by Richard M. Sherman and Robert B. Sherman

© 1963 Wonderland Music Company, Inc.
Copyright Renewed
This arrangement © 2012 Wonderland Music Company, Inc.
All Rights Reserved   Used by Permission

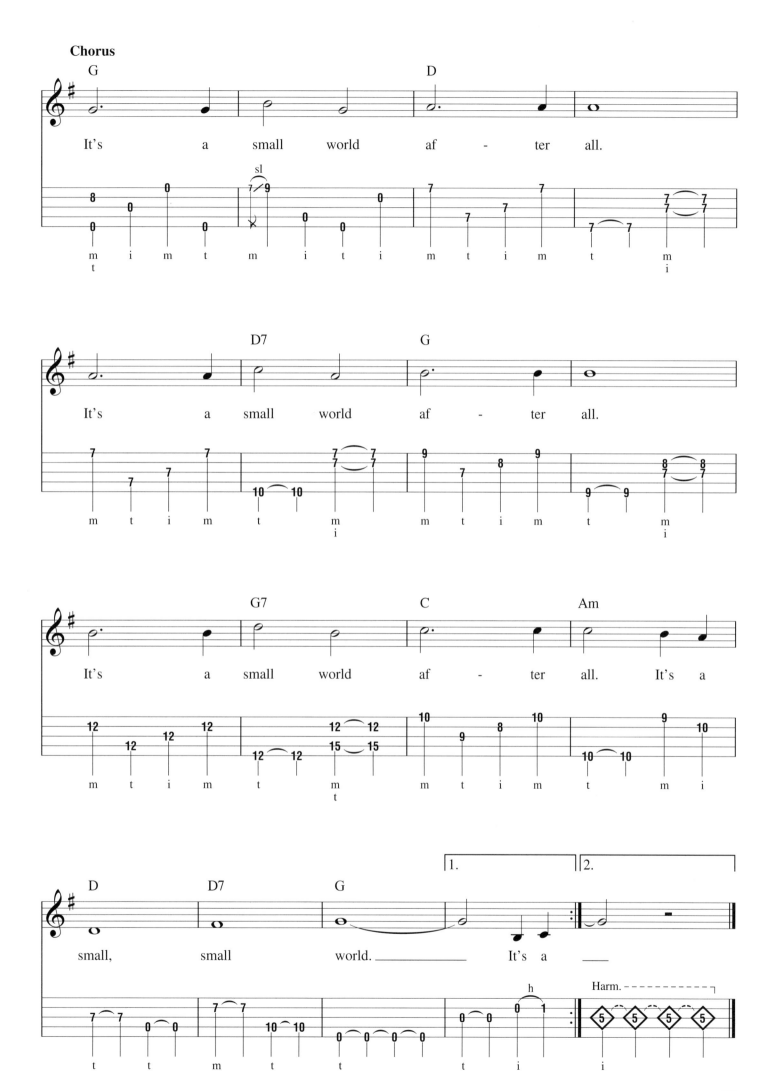

Mickey Mouse March

from Walt Disney's THE MICKEY MOUSE CLUB
Words and Music by Jimmie Dodd

© 1955 Walt Disney Music Company
Copyright Renewed
This arrangement © 2012 Walt Disney Music Company
All Rights Reserved   Used by Permission

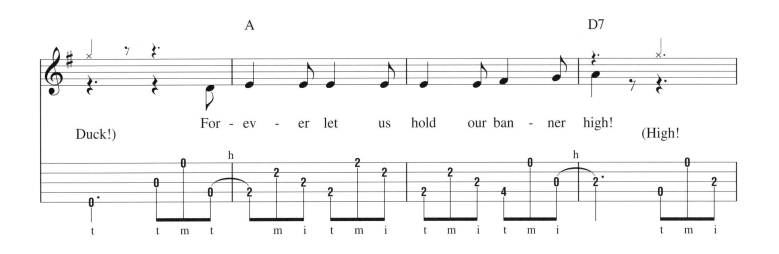

Duck!) For - ev - er let us hold our ban - ner high! (High!

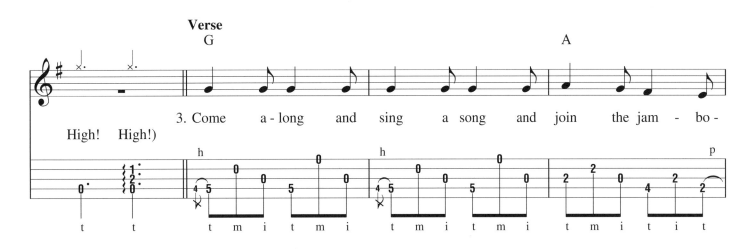

Verse

High! High!) 3. Come a - long and sing a song and join the jam - bo -

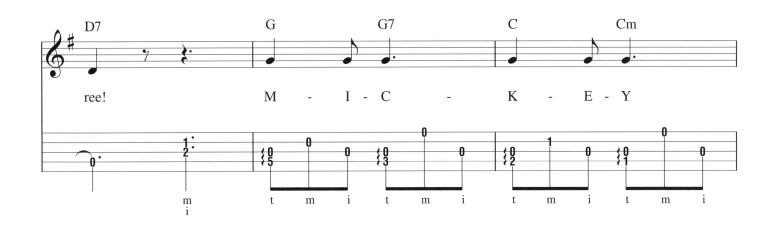

ree! M - I - C - K - E - Y

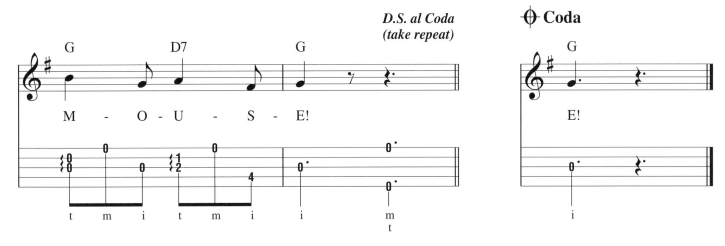

D.S. al Coda
(take repeat)

M - O - U - S - E!

Coda

E!

Supercalifragilisticexpialidocious

from Walt Disney's MARY POPPINS
Words and Music by Richard M. Sherman and Robert B. Sherman

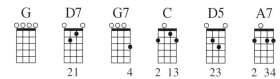

Key of G

Chorus

Fast

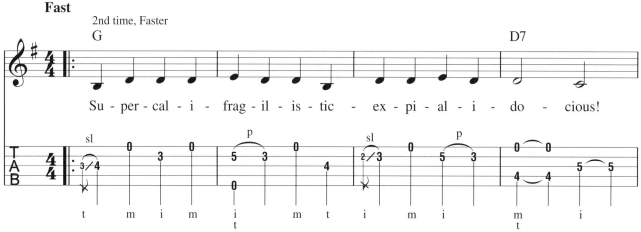

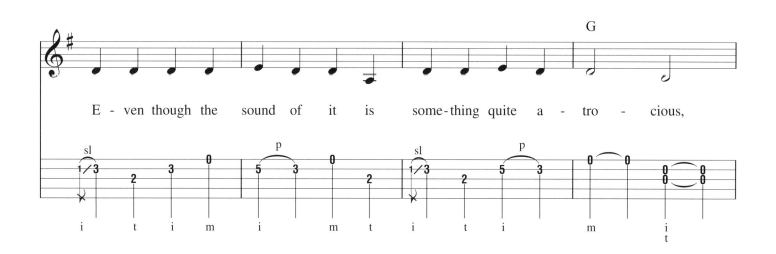

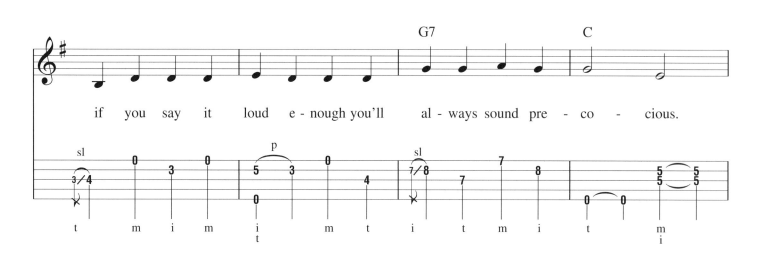

© 1963 Wonderland Music Company, Inc.
Copyright Renewed
This arrangement © 2012 Wonderland Music Company, Inc.
All Rights Reserved   Used by Permission

Bridge

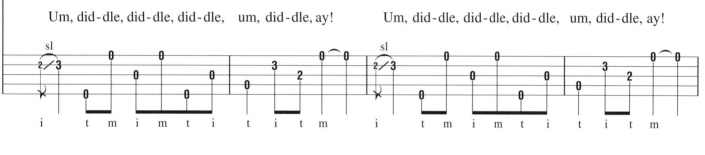

Um, did-dle, did-dle, did-dle, um, did-dle, ay! Um, did-dle, did-dle, did-dle, um, did-dle, ay!

Um, did-dle, did-dle, did-dle, um, did-dle, ay! Um, did-dle, did-dle, did-dle, um, did-dle, ay! 1. Be -
2. He
3. So

Verse

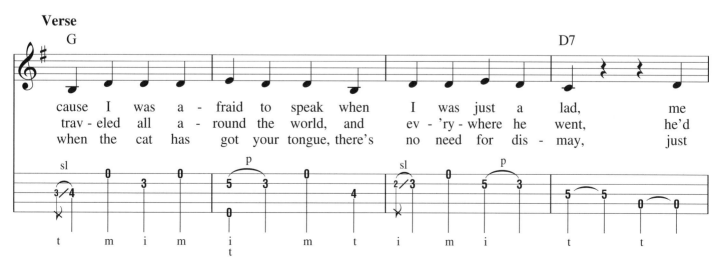

cause I was a - fraid to speak when I was just a lad, me
trav - eled all a - round the world, and ev - 'ry - where he went, he'd
when the cat has got your tongue, there's no need for dis - may, just

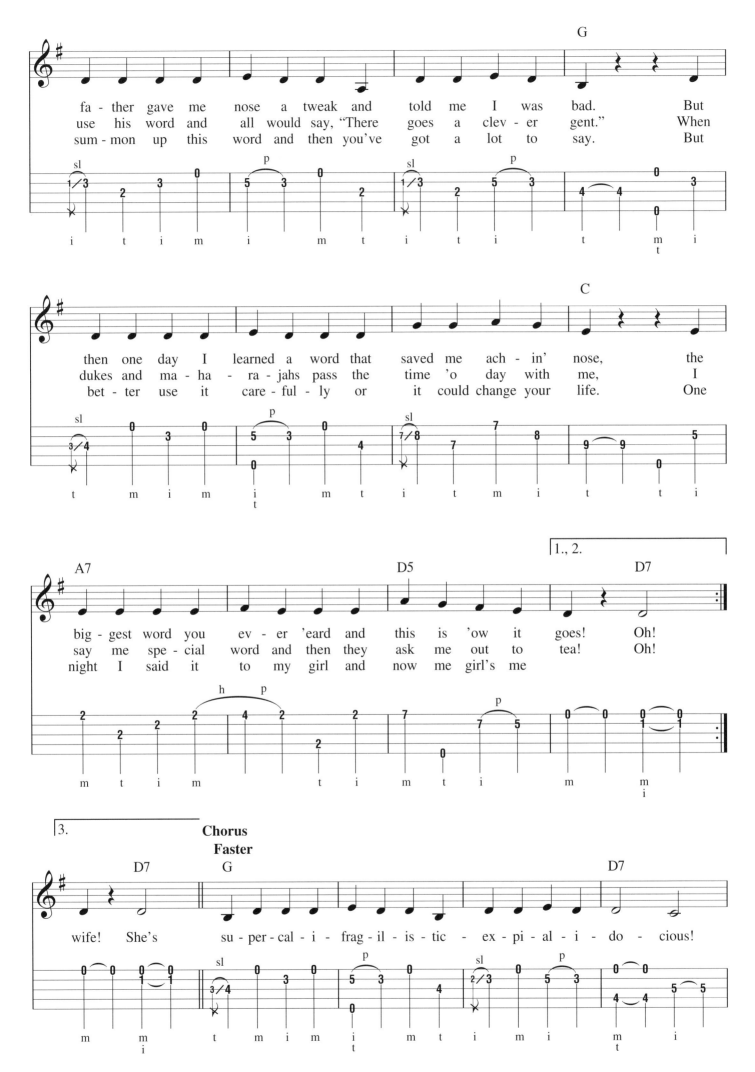

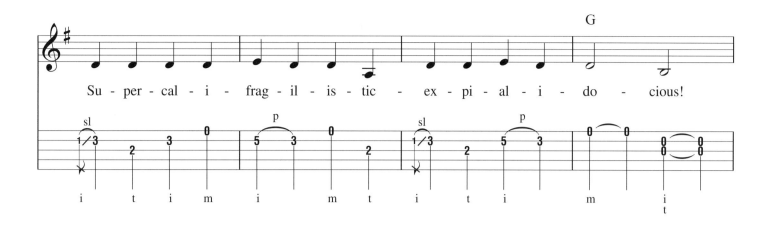

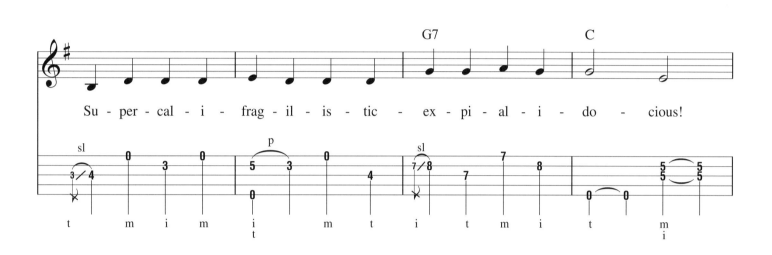

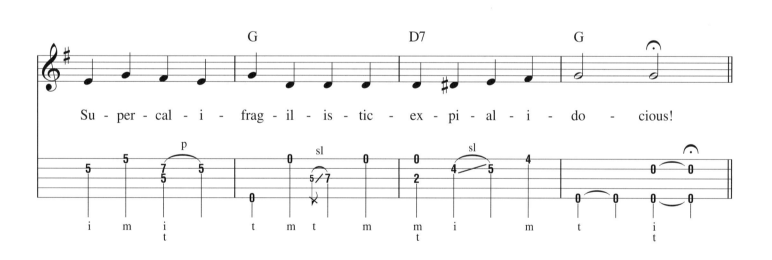

Outro-Tag
Very fast

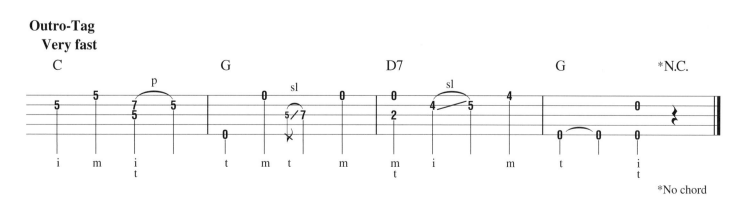

*No chord

Under the Sea

from Walt Disney's THE LITTLE MERMAID

Music by Alan Menken

Lyrics by Howard Ashman

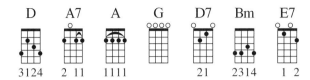

Key of D

Intro

Moderately fast

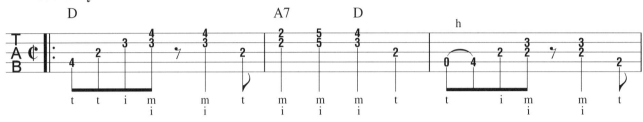

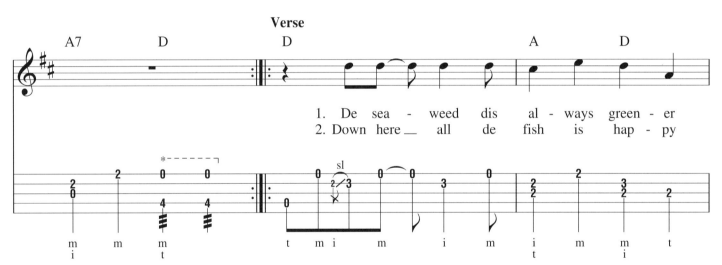

*Tremolo pick: rapidly alternate picking for two beats.

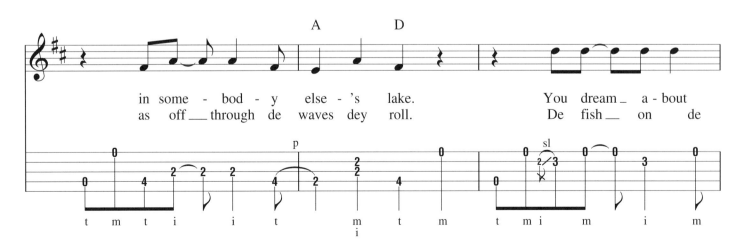

1. De sea-weed dis al-ways green-er
2. Down here __ all de fish is hap-py

in some-bod-y else-'s lake.   You dream __ a-bout
as off __ through de waves dey roll.   De fish __ on de

© 1988 Wonderland Music Company, Inc. and Walt Disney Music Company

This arrangement © 2012 Wonderland Music Company, Inc. and Walt Disney Music Company

All Rights Reserved   Used by Permission

Chorus

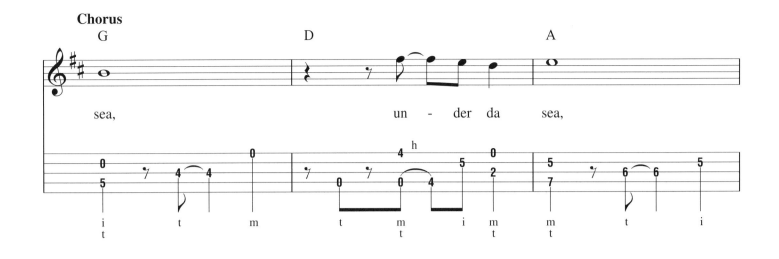

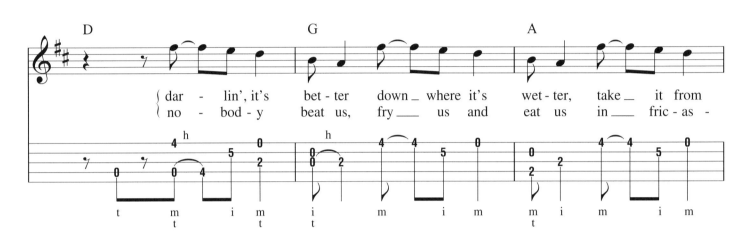

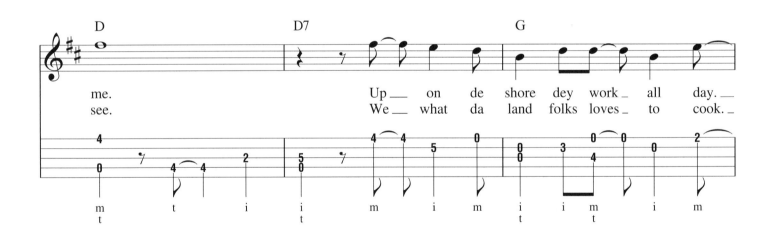

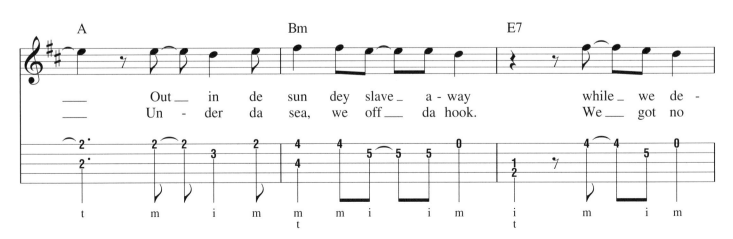

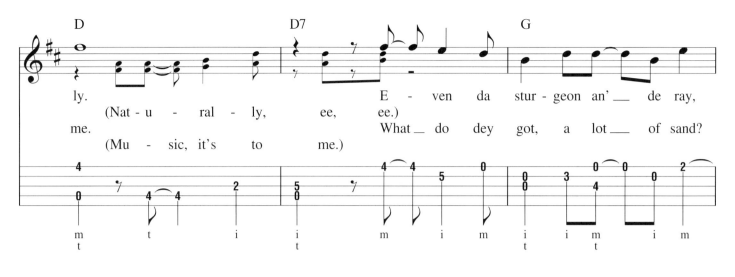

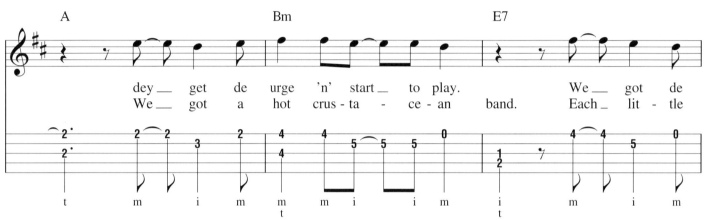

To Coda ⊕

Interlude

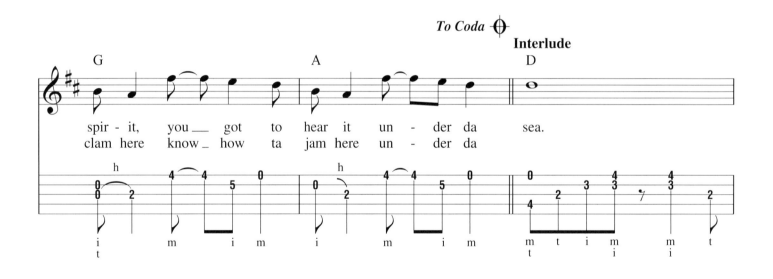

Bridge

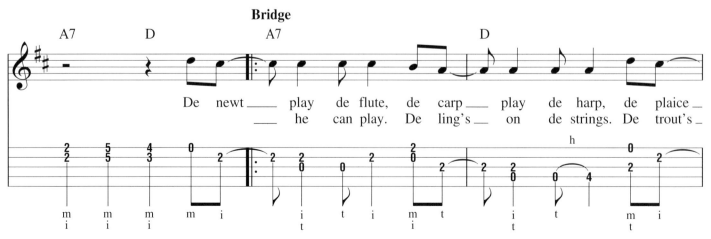

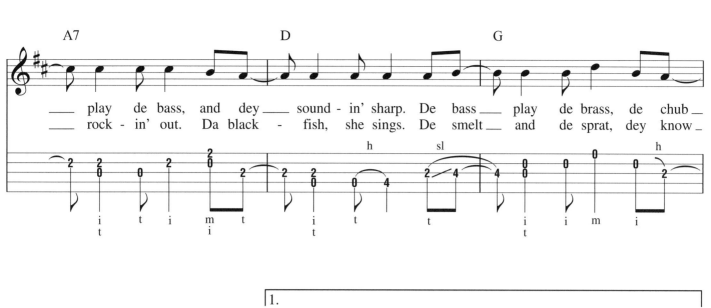

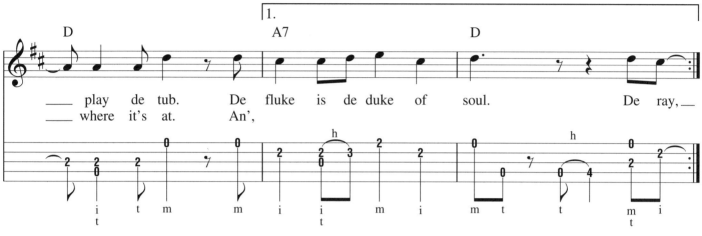

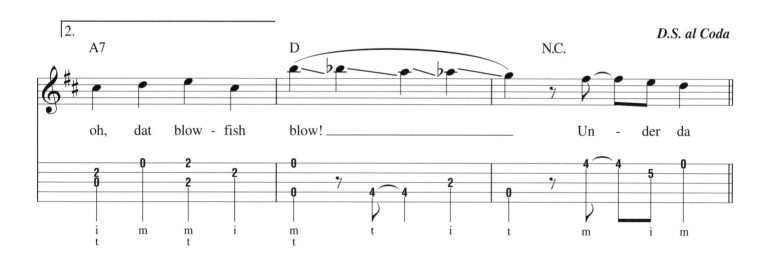

D.S. al Coda

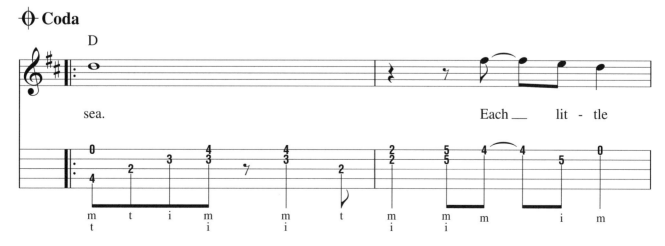

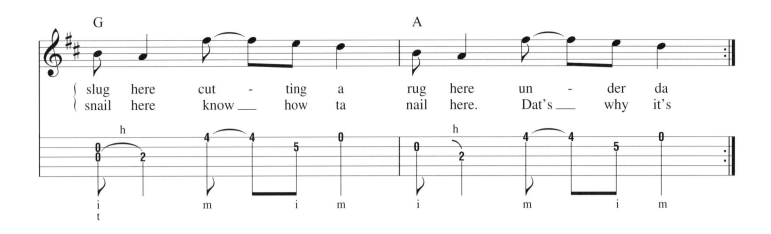

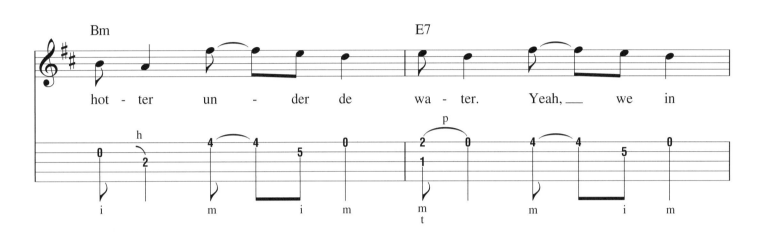

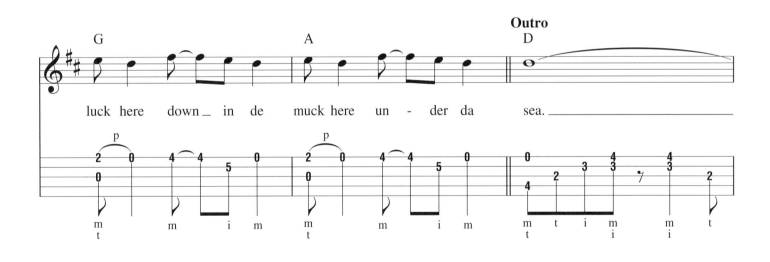

Outro

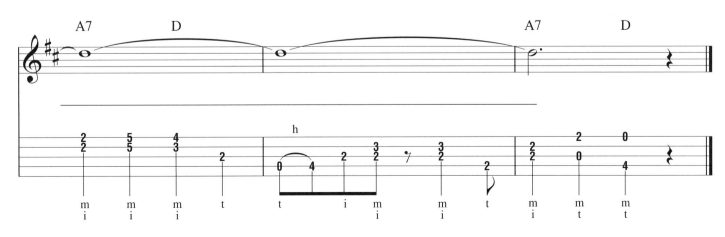

I Just Can't Wait to Be King

from Walt Disney Pictures' THE LION KING
Music by Elton John
Lyrics by Tim Rice

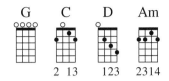

Key of G

Intro
Moderately

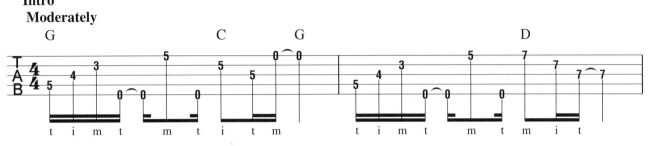

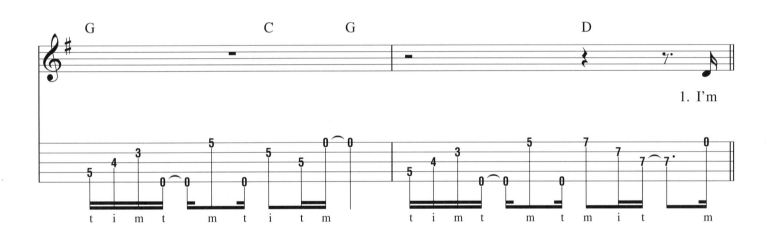

1. I'm

Verse

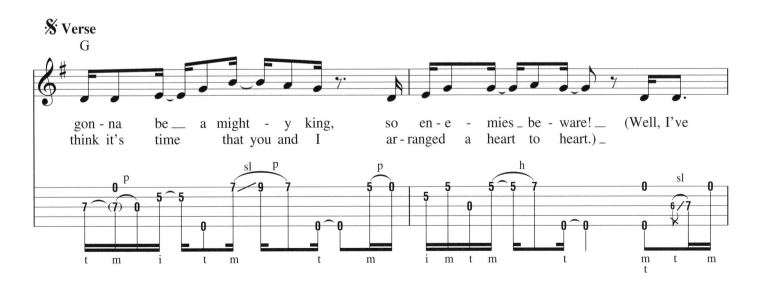

gon-na be __ a might-y king, so en-e-mies __ be-ware! __ (Well, I've
think it's time that you and I ar-ranged a heart to heart.) __

© 1994 Wonderland Music Company, Inc.
This arrangement © 2012 Wonderland Music Company, Inc.
All Rights Reserved   Used by Permission

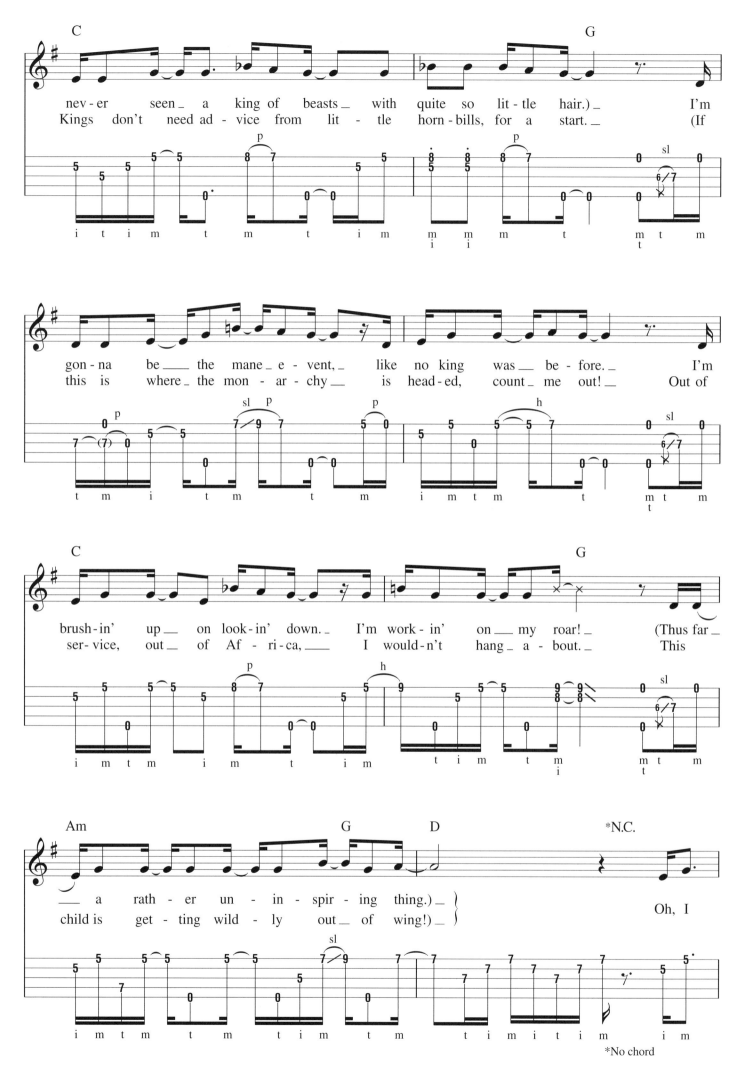

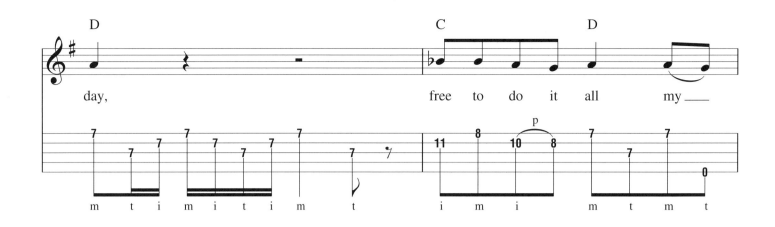

day,   free to do it all my ____

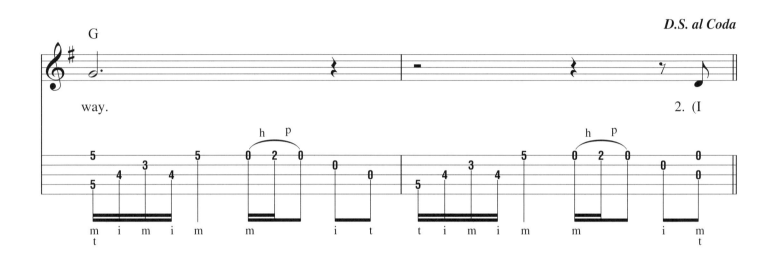

D.S. al Coda

way.   2. (I

Coda

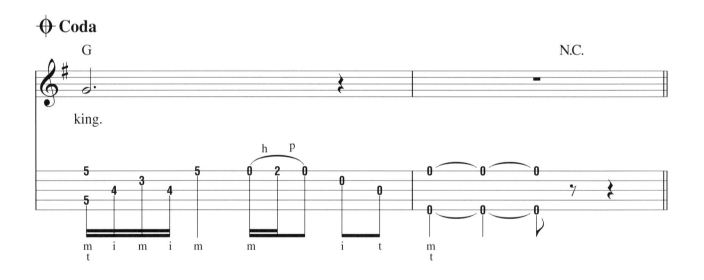

king.

N.C.

Interlude

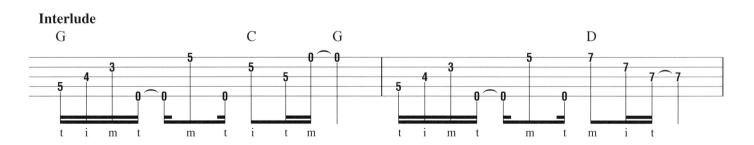

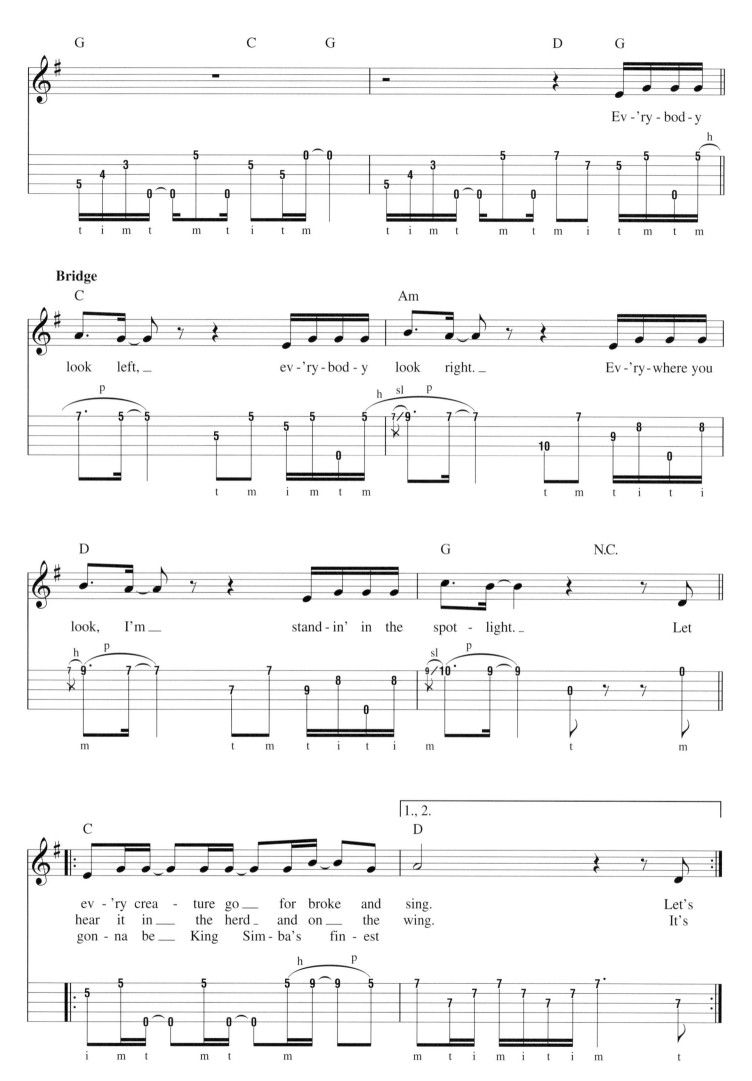

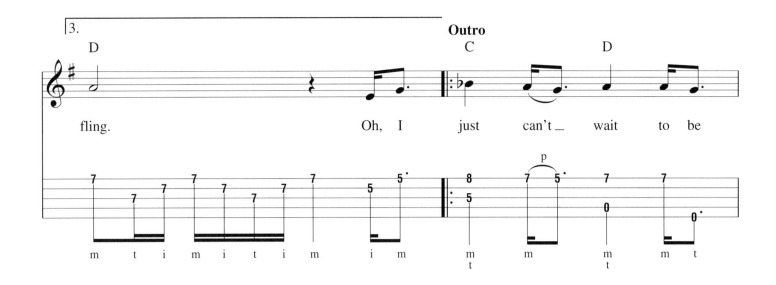

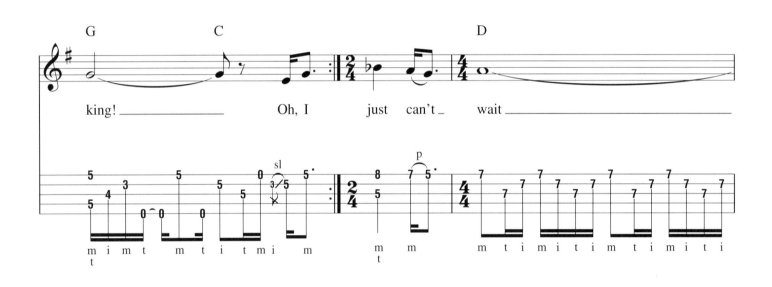

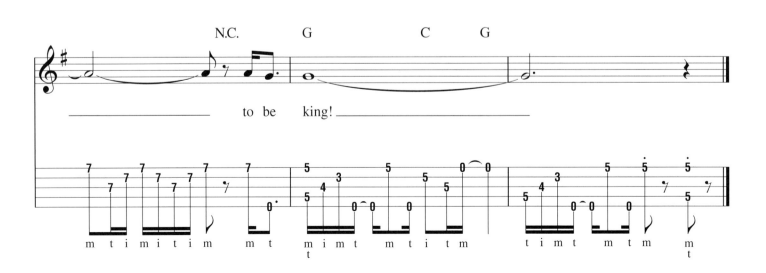

A Spoonful of Sugar

from Walt Disney's MARY POPPINS
Words and Music by Richard M. Sherman and Robert B. Sherman

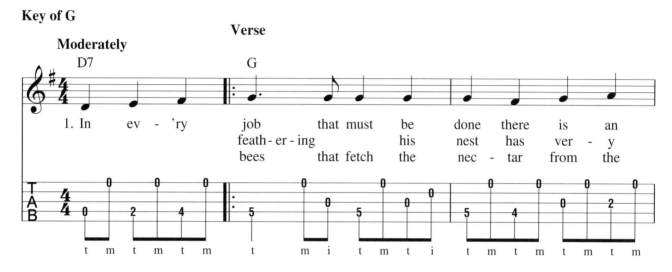

Key of G

Verse

Moderately

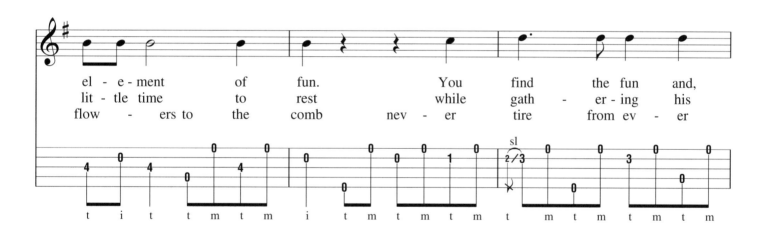

1. In ev - 'ry job that must be done there is an
feath - er - ing his nest has ver - y
bees that fetch the nec - tar from the

el - e - ment of fun. You find the fun and,
lit - tle time to rest while gath - er - ing his
flow - ers to the comb nev - er tire from ev - er

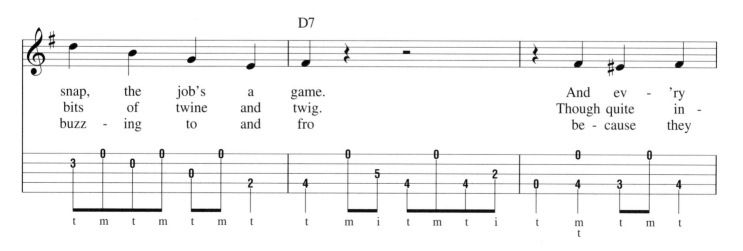

snap, the job's a game. And ev - 'ry
bits of twine and twig. Though quite in -
buzz - ing to and fro be - cause they

© 1963 Wonderland Music Company, Inc.
Copyright Renewed
This arrangement © 2012 Wonderland Music Company, Inc.
All Rights Reserved   Used by Permission

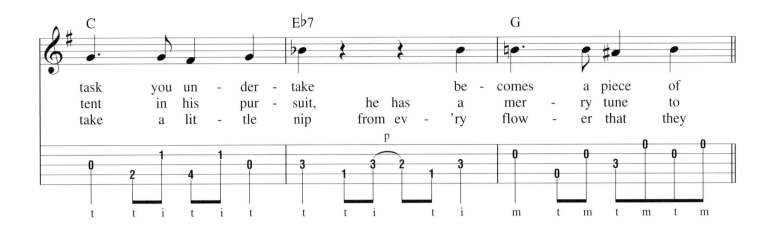

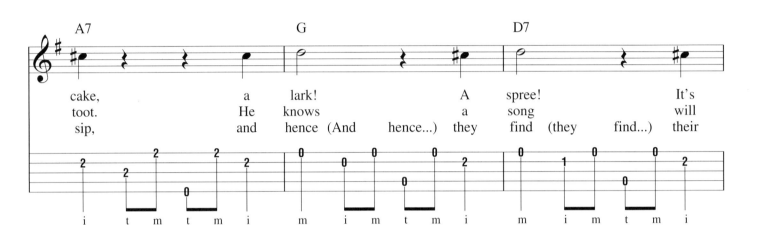

Chorus
A tempo

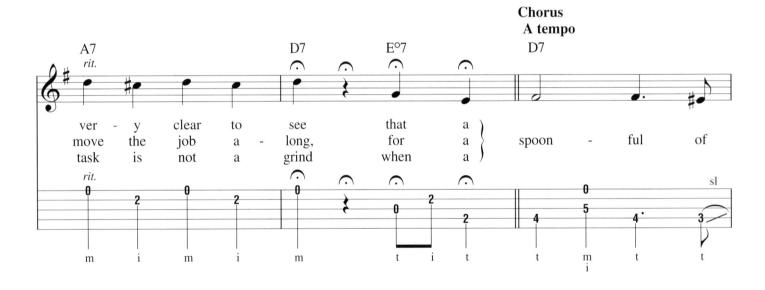

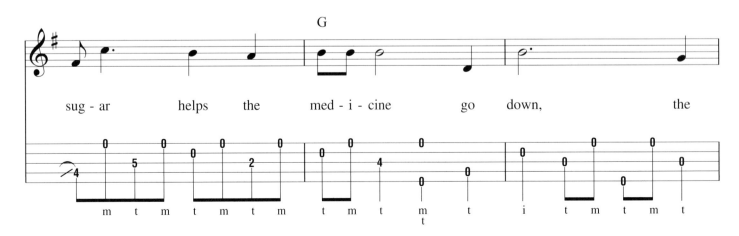

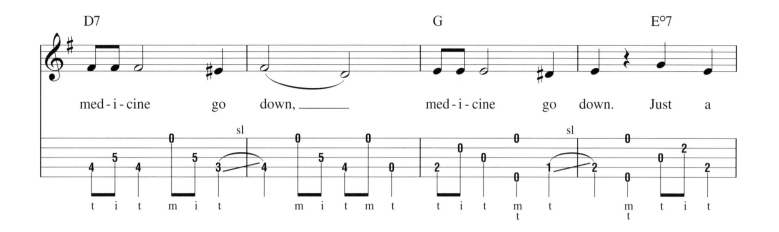

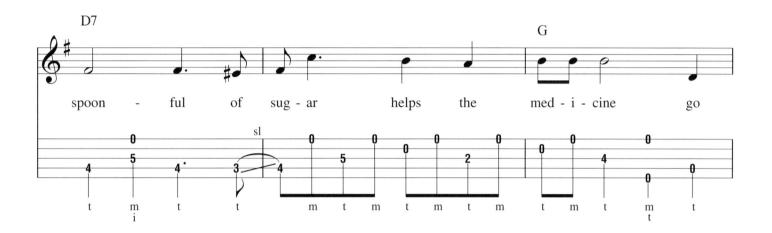

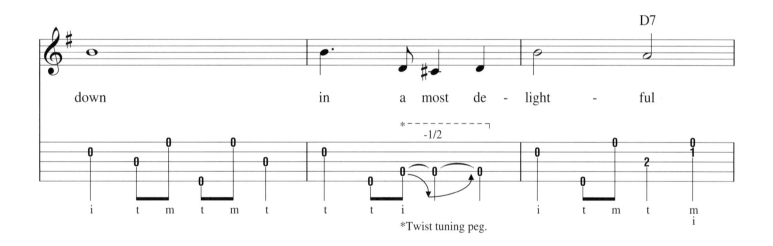

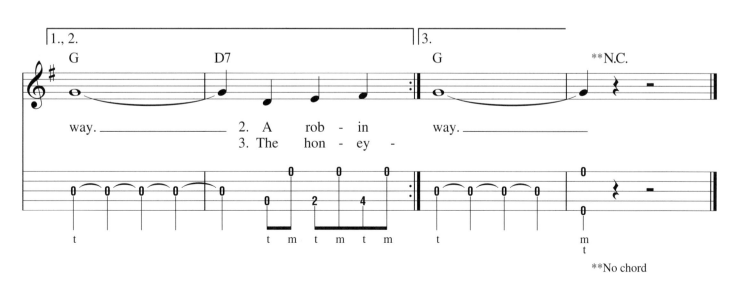

When You Wish Upon a Star

from Walt Disney's PINOCCHIO
Words by Ned Washington
Music by Leigh Harline

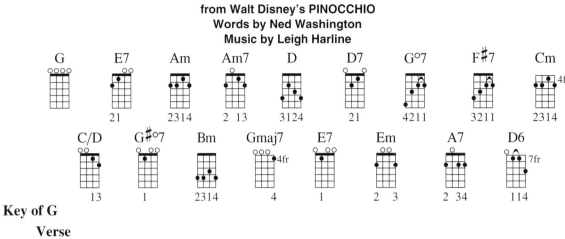

Key of G

Verse
Slow

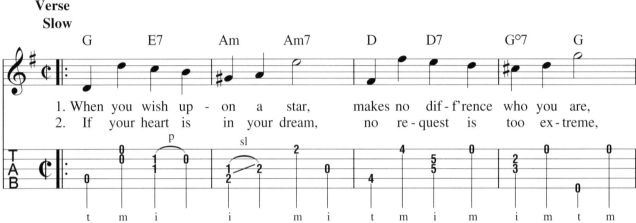

1. When you wish up - on a star, makes no dif - f'rence who you are,
2. If your heart is in your dream, no re - quest is too ex - treme,

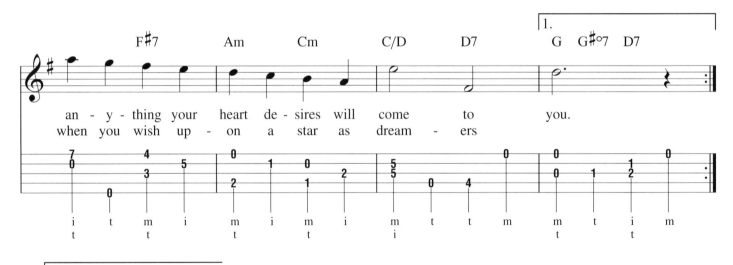

an - y - thing your heart de - sires will come to you.
when you wish up - on a star as dream - ers

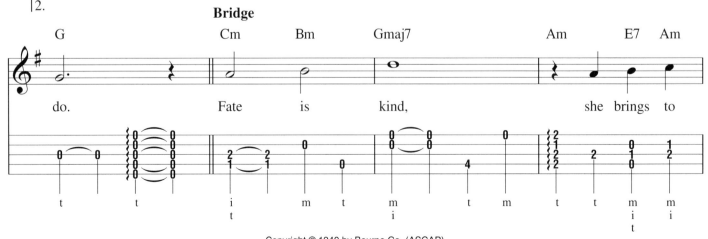

do. Fate is kind, she brings to

Copyright © 1940 by Bourne Co. (ASCAP)
Copyright Renewed
This arrangement Copyright © 2012 by Bourne Co.
International Copyright Secured   All Rights Reserved

those who love   the sweet ful - fill - ment of   the se - cret

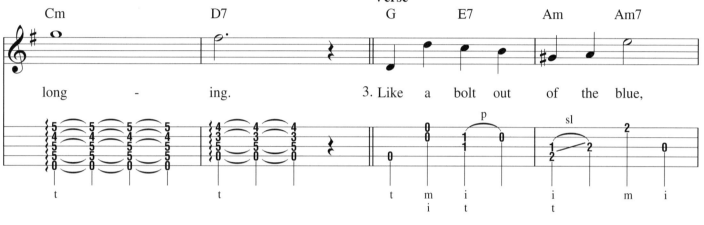

Verse

long - ing.   3. Like a bolt out of the blue,

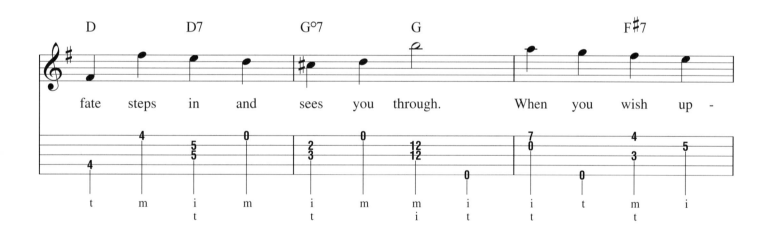

fate steps in and   sees you through.   When you wish up –

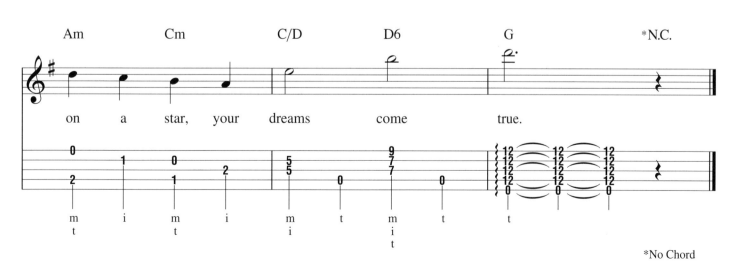

on a star, your   dreams   come   true.

*No Chord

Whistle While You Work

from Walt Disney's SNOW WHITE AND THE SEVEN DWARFS

Words by Larry Morey
Music by Frank Churchill

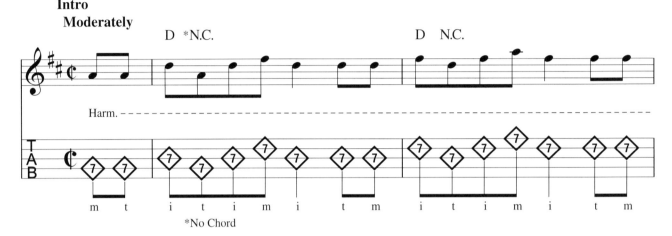

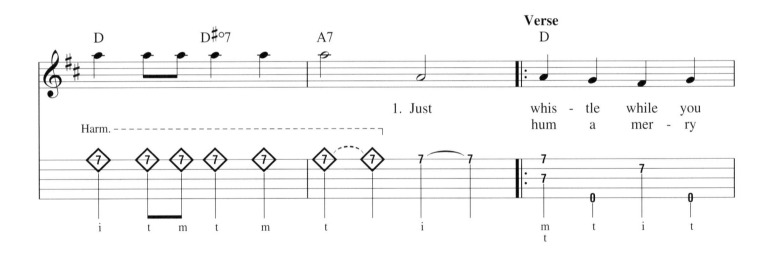

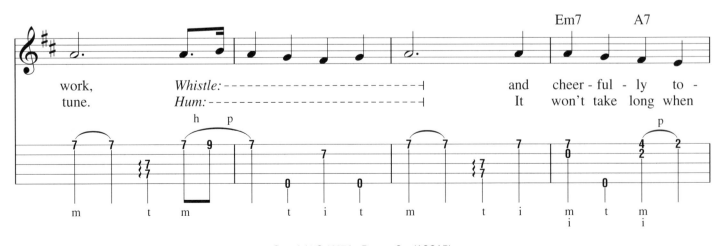

Copyright © 1937 by Bourne Co. (ASCAP)
Copyright Renewed
This arrangement Copyright © 2012 by Bourne Co.
International Copyright Secured   All Rights Reserved

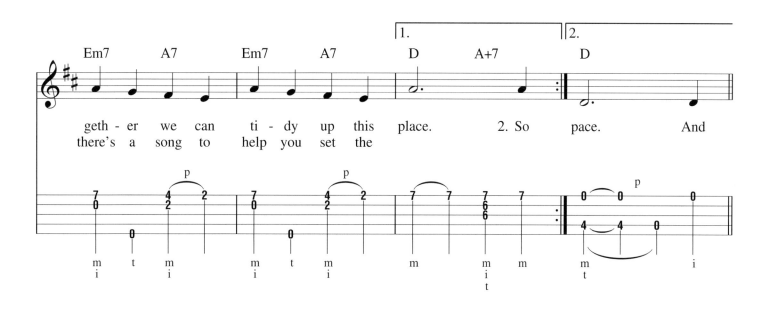

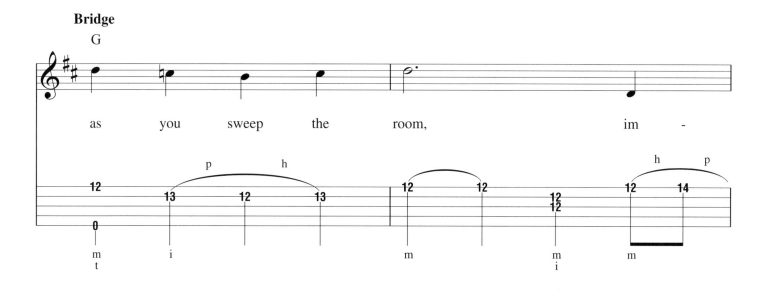

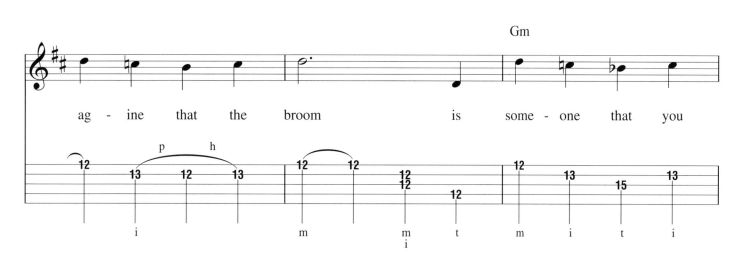

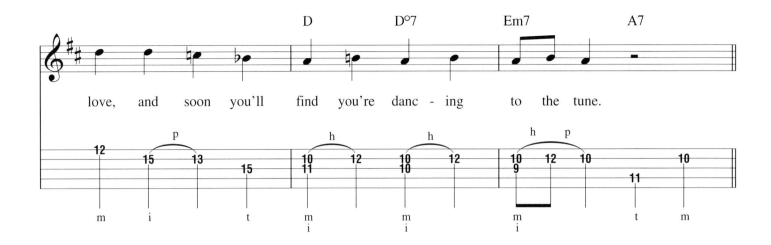

love, and soon you'll find you're danc - ing to the tune.

Verse

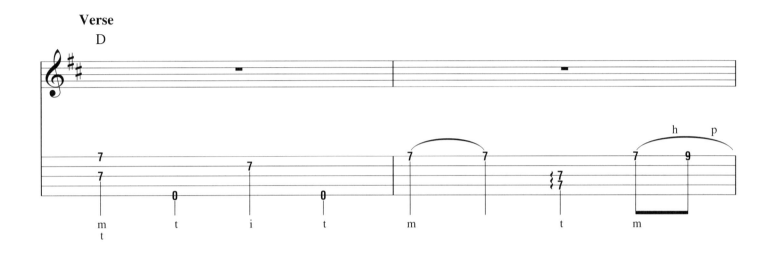

When hearts are high, the

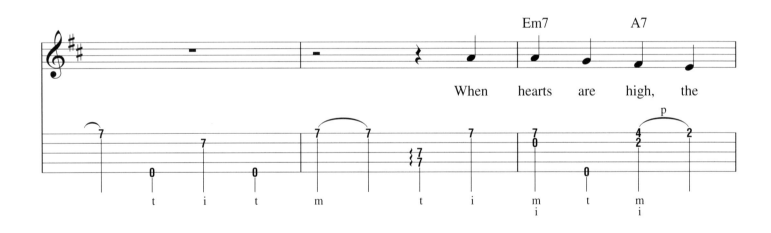

time will fly so whis - tle while you work.

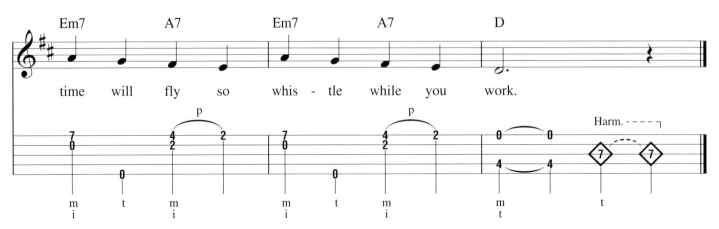

Who's Afraid of the Big Bad Wolf?

from Walt Disney's THREE LITTLE PIGS
Words and Music by Frank Churchill
Additional Lyric by Ann Ronell

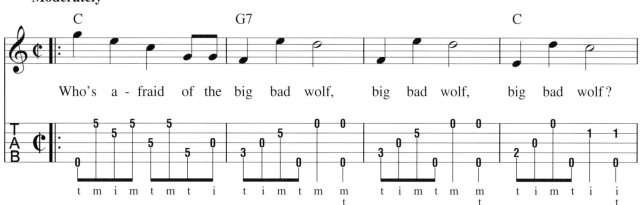

Key of C

𝄋 **Chorus**
Moderately

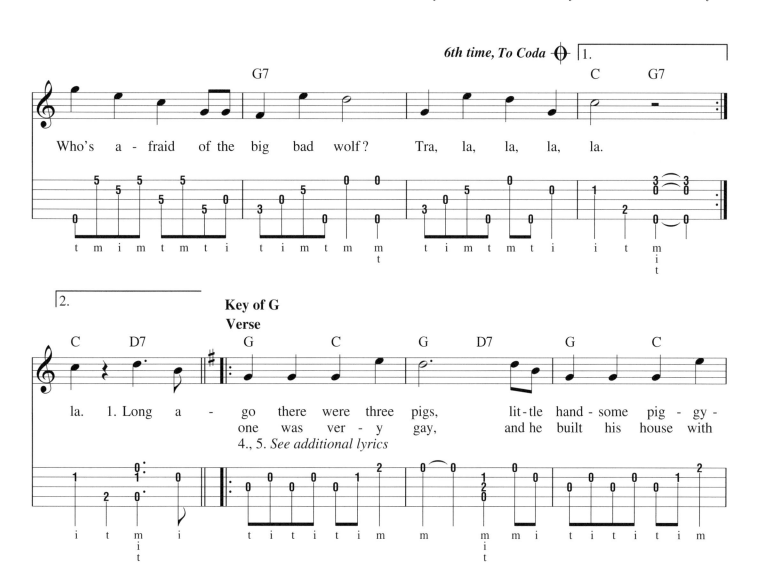

Who's a-fraid of the big bad wolf, big bad wolf, big bad wolf?

6th time, To Coda ⊕ | 1.

Who's a-fraid of the big bad wolf? Tra, la, la, la, la.

2. la. 1. Long a-go there were three pigs, lit-tle hand-some pig-gy-
one was ver-y gay, and he built his house with
4., 5. See additional lyrics

Key of G
Verse

Copyright © 1933 by Bourne Co. (ASCAP)
Copyright Renewed
This arrangement Copyright © 2012 by Bourne Co.
International Copyright Secured   All Rights Reserved

Additional Lyrics

Verse 4   Came the day when fate did frown
And the wolf blew into town.
With a gruff "puff, puff" he puffed just enough,
And the hay house fell right down.

Verse 5   One and two were scared to death
Of the big bad wolfie's breath.
"By the hair of your chinny-chin I'll blow you in."
And the twig house answered, "Yes."

Bridge 2   No one left but number three
To save the piglet family.
When they knocked, he fast unlocked
And said, "Come in with me!"

Verse 6   Now they were all safe inside,
And the bricks hurt wolfie's pride.
So he slid down the chimney and oh, by Jim'ny,
In the fire he was fried!

Winnie the Pooh

from Walt Disney's THE MANY ADVENTURES OF WINNIE THE POOH
Words and Music by Richard M. Sherman and Robert B. Sherman

© 1963 Wonderland Music Company, Inc.
Copyright Renewed
This arrangement © 2012 Wonderland Music Company, Inc.
All Rights Reserved   Used by Permission

You've Got a Friend in Me

from Walt Disney's TOY STORY
Music and Lyrics by Randy Newman

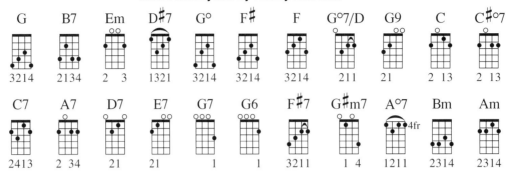

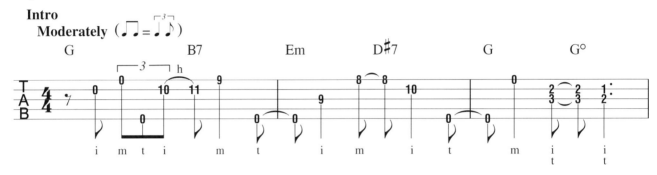

Key of G

Intro
Moderately

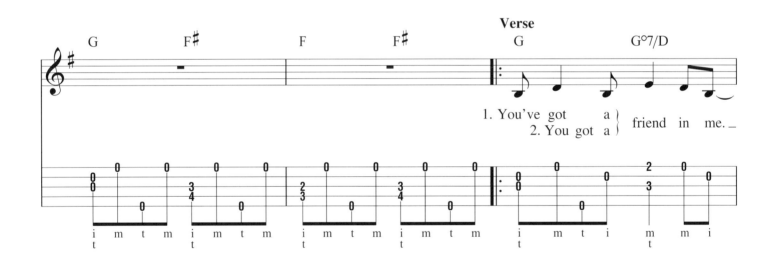

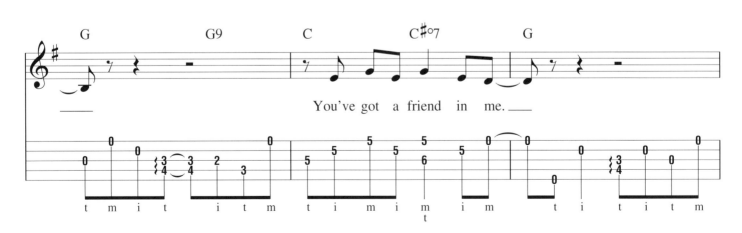

1. You've got a friend in me.
2. You got a friend in me.

You've got a friend in me.

© 1995 Walt Disney Music Company
This arrangement © 2012 Walt Disney Music Company
All Rights Reserved   Used by Permission

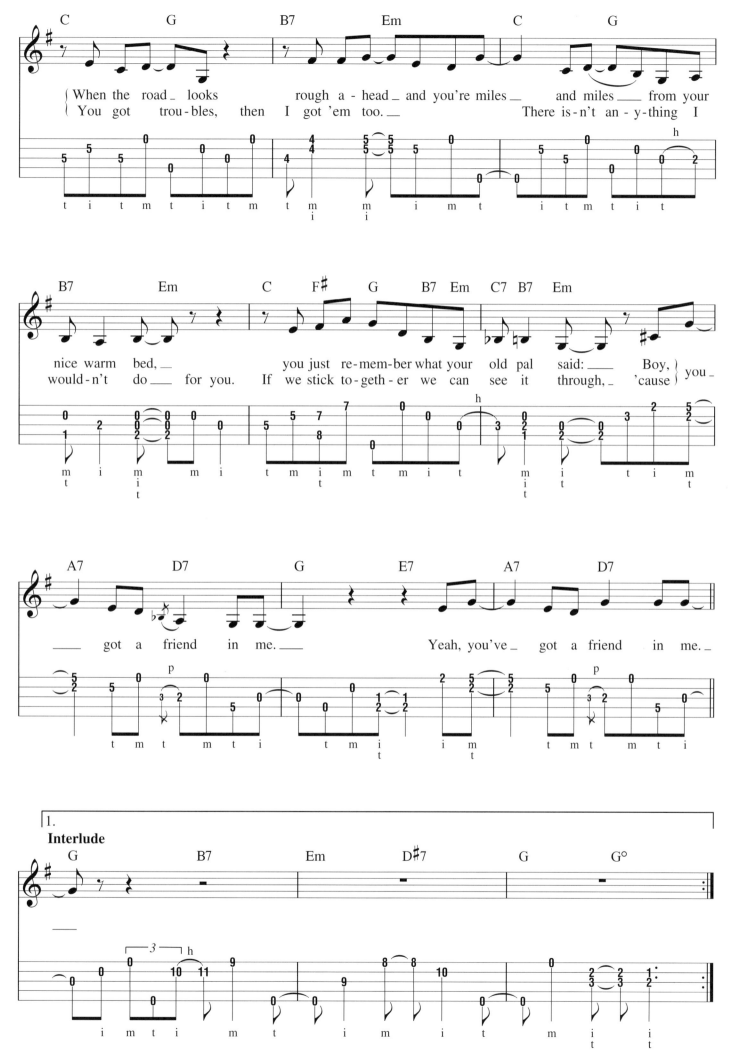

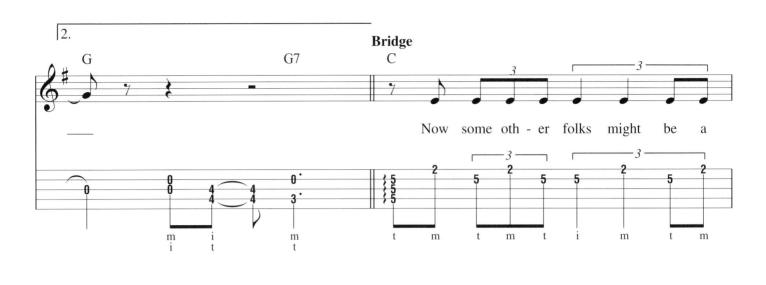

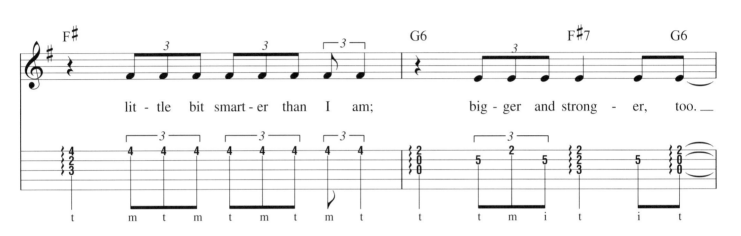

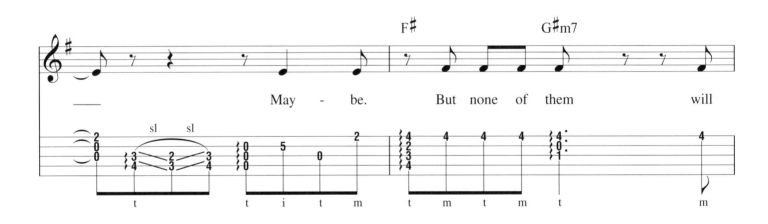

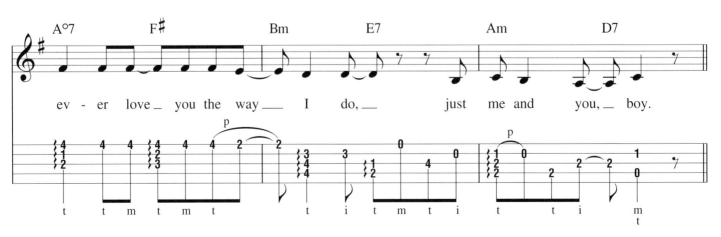

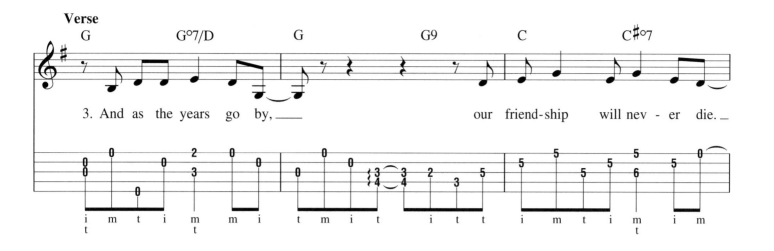

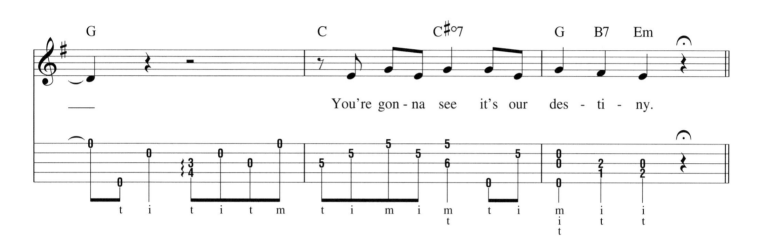

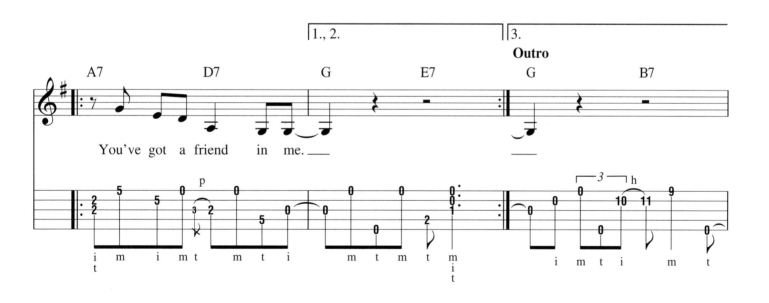

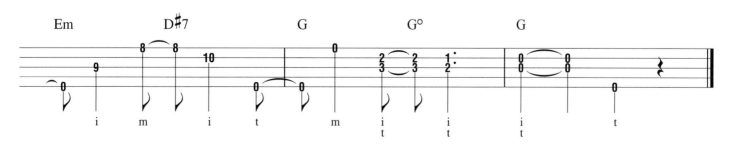

Zip-A-Dee-Doo-Dah

from Walt Disney's SONG OF THE SOUTH
Words by Ray Gilbert
Music by Allie Wrubel

© 1945 Walt Disney Music Company
Copyright Renewed
This arrangement © 2012 Walt Disney Music Company
All Rights Reserved   Used by Permission

Bridge

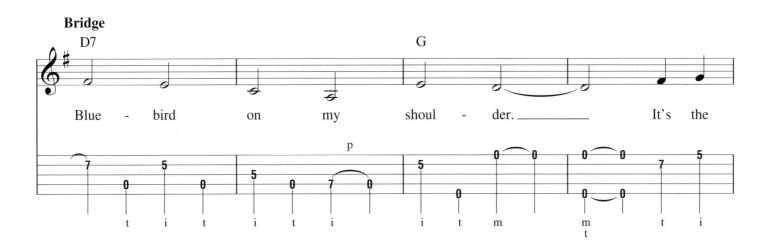

Blue - bird on my shoul - der. _____ It's the

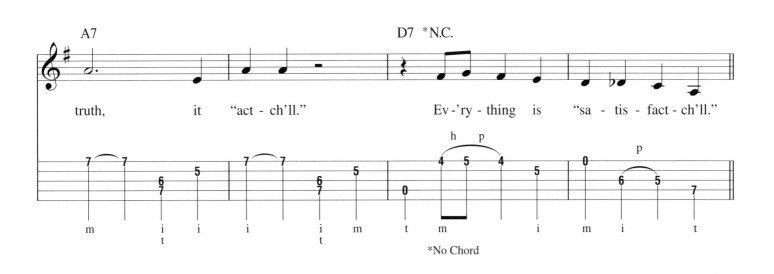

truth, it "act - ch'll." Ev -'ry - thing is "sa - tis - fact - ch'll."

*No Chord

Verse

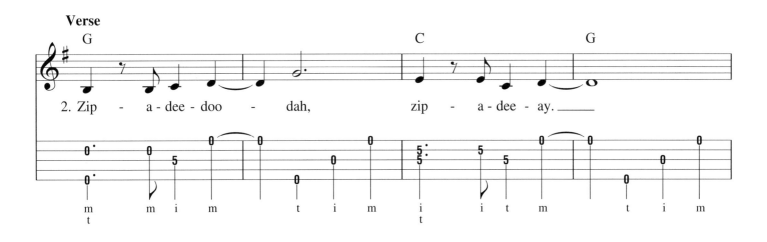

2. Zip - a - dee - doo - dah, zip - a - dee - ay. _____

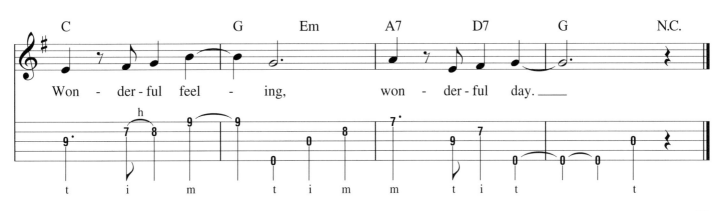

Won - der - ful feel - ing, won - der - ful day. _____

You'll Be in My Heart

from Walt Disney Pictures' TARZAN™
Words and Music by Phil Collins

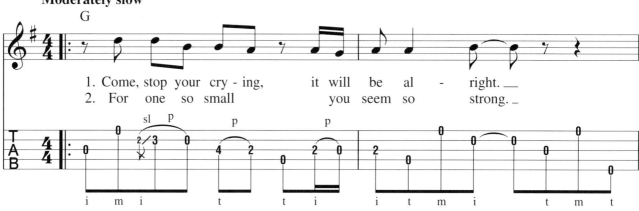

Key of G

Verse
Moderately slow

1. Come, stop your cry - ing, it will be al - right. __
2. For one so small you seem so strong. _

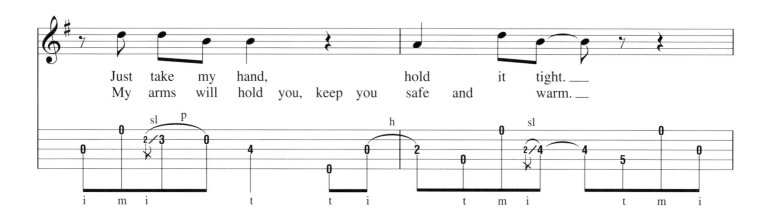

Just take my hand, hold it tight. __
My arms will hold you, keep you safe and warm. _

I will pro - tect you from all a - round __ you.
This bond be - tween us can't be bro - ken.

© 1999 Edgar Rice Burroughs, Inc. and Walt Disney Music Company
This arrangement © 2012 Edgar Rice Burroughs, Inc. and Walt Disney Music Company
All Rights Reserved   Used by Permission

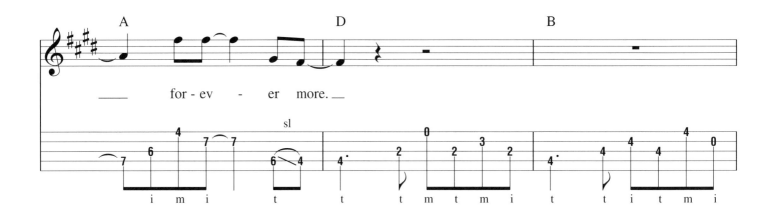

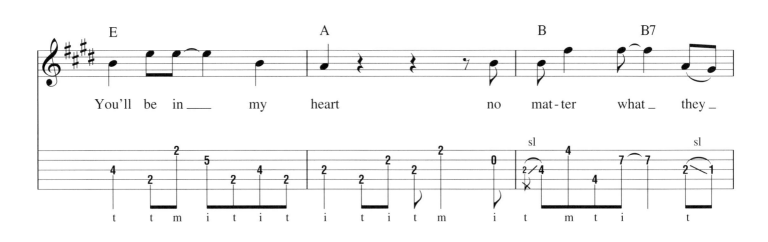

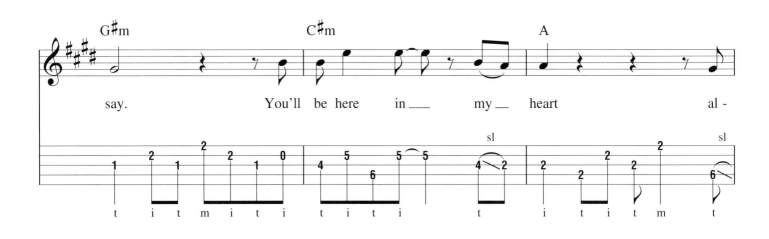

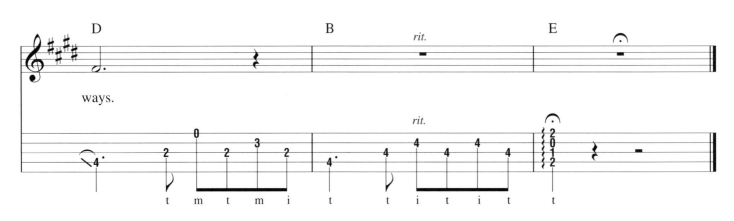

BANJO NOTATION LEGEND

TABLATURE graphically represents the banjo fingerboard. Each horizontal line represents a string, and each number represents a fret.

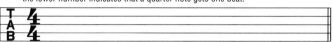

4th string, 2nd fret

1st & 2nd strings open, played together

TIME SIGNATURE:
The upper number indicates the number of beats per measure, the lower number indicates that a quarter note gets one beat.

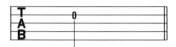

CUT TIME:
Each note's time value should be cut in half. As a result, the music will be played twice as fast as it is written.

QUARTER NOTE:
time value = 1 beat

EIGHTH NOTES:
time value = 1/2 beat each

single   in series

SIXTEENTH NOTES:
time value = 1/4 beat each

single   in series

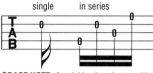

DOTTED QUARTER NOTE:
time value = 1 1/2 beat

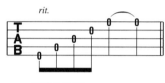

TIE: Pick the 1st note only, then let it sustain for the combined time value.

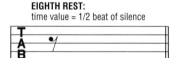

TRIPLET: Three notes played in the same time normally occupied by two notes of the same time value.

GRACE NOTE: A quickly played note with no time value of its own. The grace note and the note following it only occupy the time value of the second note.

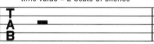

RITARD: A gradual slowing of the tempo or speed of the song.

rit.

QUARTER REST:
time value = 1 beat of silence

EIGHTH REST:
time value = 1/2 beat of silence

HALF REST:
time value = 2 beats of silence

WHOLE REST:
time value = 4 beats of silence

ENDINGS: When a repeated section has a first and second ending, play the first ending only the first time and play the second ending only the second time.

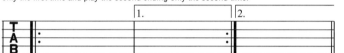

REPEAT SIGNS: Play the music between the repeat signs two times.

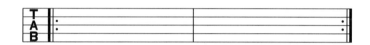

D.S. AL CODA:
Play through the music until you complete the measure labeled *"D.S. al Coda,"* then go back to the sign (%).
Then play until you complete the measure labeled *"To Coda* ⊕ *,"* then skip to the section labeled *"* ⊕ *Coda."*

%   *To Coda* ⊕   *D.S. al Coda*   ⊕ *Coda*

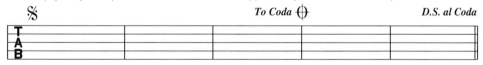

HAMMER-ON: Strike the first (lower) note with one finger, then sound the higher note (on the same string) with another finger by fretting it without picking.

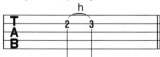

PULL-OFF: Place both fingers on the notes to be sounded. Strike the first note and without picking, pull the finger off to sound the second (lower) note.

SLIDE UP: Strike the first note and then slide the same fret-hand finger up to the second note. The second note is not struck.

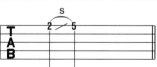

SLIDE DOWN: Strike the first note and then slide the same fret-hand finger down to the second note. The second note is not struck.

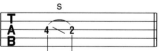

HALF-STEP CHOKE: Strike the note and bend the string up 1/2 step.

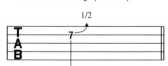

WHOLE-STEP CHOKE: Strike the note and bend the string up one step.

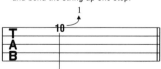

NATURAL HARMONIC: Strike the note while the fret-hand lightly touches the string directly over the fret indicated.

Harm.

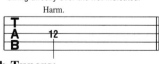

BRUSH: Play the notes of the chord indicated by quickly rolling them from bottom to top.

Scruggs/Keith Tuners:

HALF-TWIST UP: Strike the note, twist tuner up 1/2 step, and continue playing.

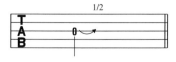

HALF-TWIST DOWN: Strike the note, twist tuner down 1/2 step, and continue playing.

WHOLE-TWIST UP: Strike the note, twist tuner up one step, and continue playing.

WHOLE-TWIST DOWN: Strike the note, twist tuner down one step, and continue playing.

Right Hand Fingerings

t = thumb   i = index finger   m = middle finger